Folksinger 101

Author   **Steve Ono 2023**

ISBN: 9798853792265

Folksinger 101 Basic Guitar Skills

Contents

Guitar Parts	3
Tuning: The 5th & 4th Frets	4
A Major or "A" and E Major or "E"	5
The Musical ABCs and Neck Map	6
4 Fingers 4 Frets	7
Open C and G7	8
The Key of C major	9
Two Kinds of A chords: Major and Minor	11
Eighth Notes	11
Guide Fingers	13
Four Fretting Strategies	14
Three Chord Rock	15
Stock Changes	16
V Can Be **V7** / Dominant Seventh	17
Dominant Seventh and the Blues	17
Triplets & Compound Meter	18
First Review	19
Notes on the 1st and 2nd String	21
Yet Another Mystery Tune	22
Flats, Sharps & Naturals	23
Dots & Ties	24
Notes on the 3rd & 4th Strings	25
More Flats & Sharps	25
More Mystery Tunes	26
Notes on the 5th & 6th Strings	28
Bass Lines	30

Walk Up and Walk Down Bass Line	30
The Major Minor Yin Yang	31
Chord Numbers	32
Changing the Key with Capos	32
Cheap Tricks	33
PIMA	34
Travis Picking (outside-inside roll)	36
Open Power Chords & The Blues	37
The Shuffle and Swing	38
Moveable Power Chords	39
Sixteenth Notes	39
Rests and Left-hand Muting	40
Muting	41
Expression and More Musical Symbols	41
C/Am Pentatonic Scale	42
Seventh Chords	43
Passing Chords/ Inversion	44
Popular Rhythms	45
Bar Chords	45
Three Ways to Learn a Song	46
Finding the Notes	47
Finding the Chords	49
Keys / The Circle of 5ths	52
The Major Key and Minor Key Spelling Charts	53
Final Review	54
Note Guide for Guitar	56

Folksinger 101 Basic Guitar Skills

Guitar Parts

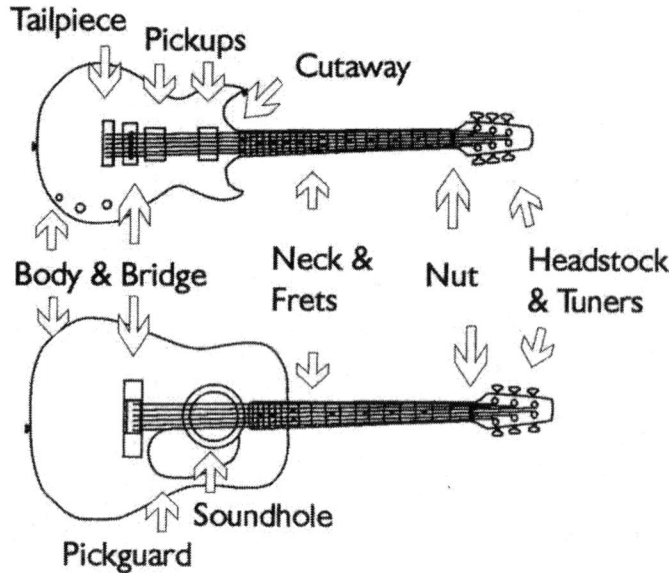

Headstock, Neck & Body The headstock is where the tuning machines are placed.

The neck has a fingerboard with frets under the six strings forming a grid from the nut to the end of the fingerboard to the bridge.

The body is the hollow amplifier in acoustic guitars. Acoustics have a sound hole, which is replaced by the pickups on a solid body electric guitar.

Fingering Touch the string as close to the fret as possible with the fingertip only. Keep your knuckles arched, fingers spread apart and your thumb at the back of the neck (not hooked over the top!). One finger one fret.

Squeeze the string to the neck as lightly as you can & still get the sound. No floppy fingertips! We want clear sustained notes with no buzzing strings!

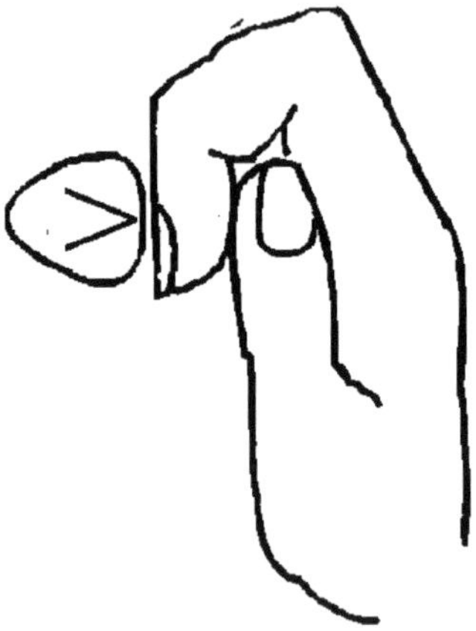

Holding the Pick Hold the pick between the thumb & side of forefinger.

"Picking" is plucking individual notes on individual strings one at a time.

"Strumming" is striking two or more strings. Pick each string down / up then strum the whole chord down / up.

Fingerpicking: The Classical Guitar fingering system is PIMA: pulgar, indice, medio y anular; Spanish for thumb, index, middle and ring. The lower string bass notes are thumb territory and the higher string's notes are finger territory.

The thumb and fingers can also pinch lower and higher strings simultaneously while leaving strings in between un-played. A real advantage over a pick.

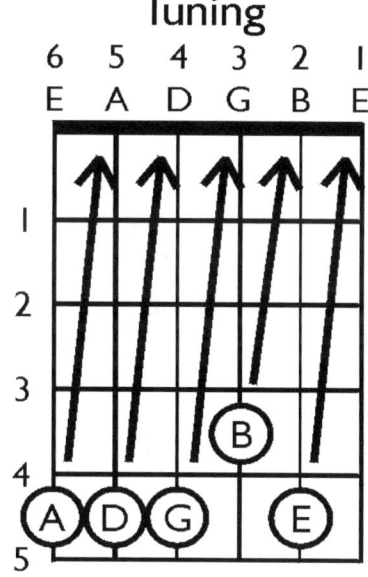

Tuning: The 5th & 4th Frets

Eddie Ate Dynamite Good-Bye Eddie. EADGBE
Electronic tuners are great devices, but you need to know the names of the strings and how to tune by ear. The strings are numbered 1 through 6, from skinny to thick and the frets are numbered from the nut to the sound hole.

In standard tuning each string is tuned to the note at the 5th fret of the lower string except the 2nd string which is tuned from the 3rd string 4th fret "B".

Turn the tuners clockwise for higher pitch and counterclockwise for lower pitch.

The Wobble or Wave

Tune the low "E" string to a tuner or a piano. Press the 6th string down at the 5th fret. Pick that note and the open 5th string and let them ring together. Listen for the "wobble". This sound is always present when strings are out of tune. As the two pitches become closer the wobble becomes slower like a wave. If they are farther apart and the "wobble" becomes faster.

<u>**The first question:**</u> **Is it out of tune?** If the two strings "wobble" at all, the answer is yes! If it is a slow wave, you are very close!

<u>**The second question:**</u> **Is it too high or too low?** Is it sharp or flat?

Hint #1) Sing each of the strings' notes and listen to the pitch of your own voice.
Hint #2) Listen to changes in the speed of the "wobble".
Hint #3) Turn the tuning machine with your right hand and listen for the speed change.

Do not turn the tuner unless you can hear the string it adjusts. Otherwise, you can't tell where it went.

Remember: slower is closer, faster is farther apart.
      When the wave stops you are in tune!

If you can sing in tune, you can already hear and understand musical elements. You just don't know what things are named and how they are organized yet.

Folksinger 101 Basic Guitar Skills

A Major or "A" and E Major or "E"

Keep your fingertips on the fingerboard. Don't fall over!

Finger hopping

Change the chord from A to E as follows:

1. Lift the first finger.
2. Hop the second & third fingers together to 5th & 4th strings.
3. Place the first finger on the 3rd string at the 1st fret. Then reverse it: E to A.

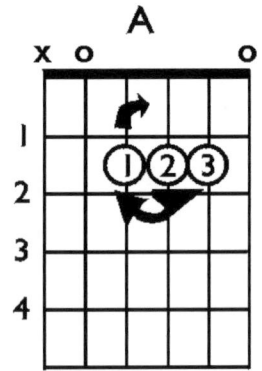
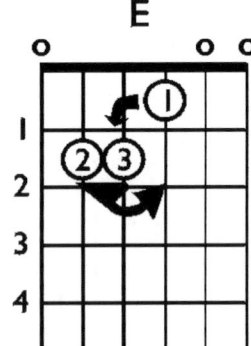

4/4 Time and Beat Counting

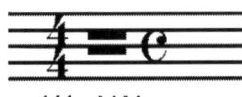

4/4 AKA
Common Time
4 Beats
Quarter Note

The "common" time signature is "C" or "4/4" meaning four quarter notes per measure or bar. The top number indicates "How many" notes. The bottom number tells us "What kind" of note gets the beat count. If the tempo (speed) is slow, you should be able to make the chord change on time for the next beat.

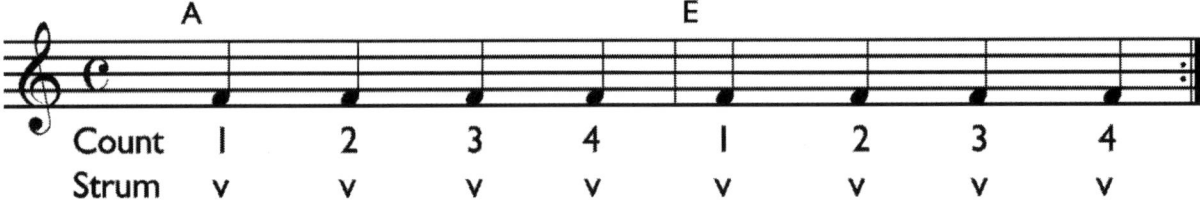

Make the Changes/Stay on the Beat

1) Tap your foot and count to four over and over very slowly.

2) Strum the A chord four times and change quickly to the E chord. Strum with your wrist, not your elbow.

3) Strum the E chord four times and change back. Keep the count very slow so you have more time to change chords quickly between beat number "four" and beat "One". Repeat these and all exercises 50 to 100 times.

Can you hear any songs to sing with those chords? Mary Had a Little Lamb?

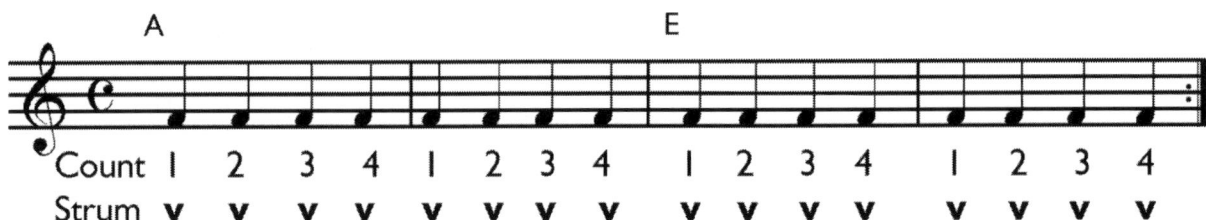

The Musical ABCs and Neck Map

ABCDEFG going up and GFEDCBA going down in whole steps and half steps, two frets and one fret.

Music notes are arranged in patterns of "intervals" (distance between notes). The two smallest intervals are a "half step or minor 2nd" (1 fret) and "whole step or major 2nd" (2 frets).

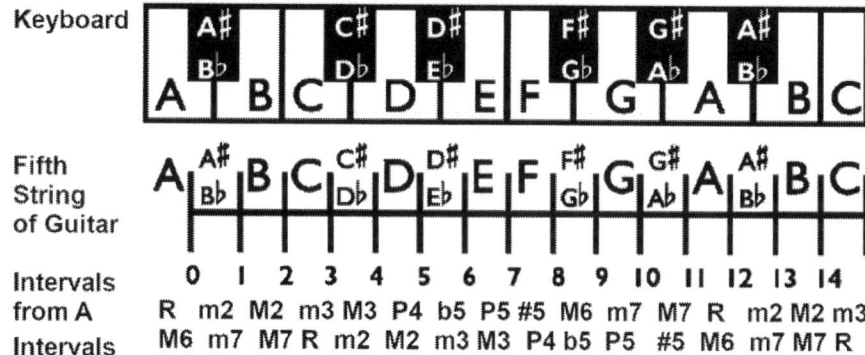

White dots are white keys.
Every natural note is a whole step apart except E & F and B & C. There are only two natural half steps.
The black dots are black keys.
The black key or dot between each pair of natural notes is called the sharp of the note below (# meaning "higher") or the flat of the note above (b meaning "lower").

Think of the neck of the guitar as six long main streets (strings) and twelve cross streets (frets). At each intersection (address) a note lives!
Copy the natural notes and sing them by name.
Singing is ear training.

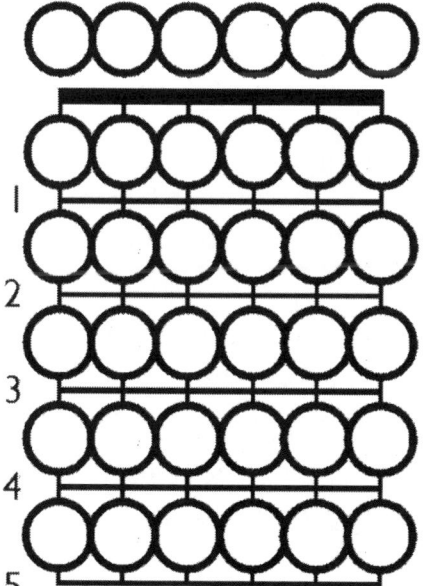

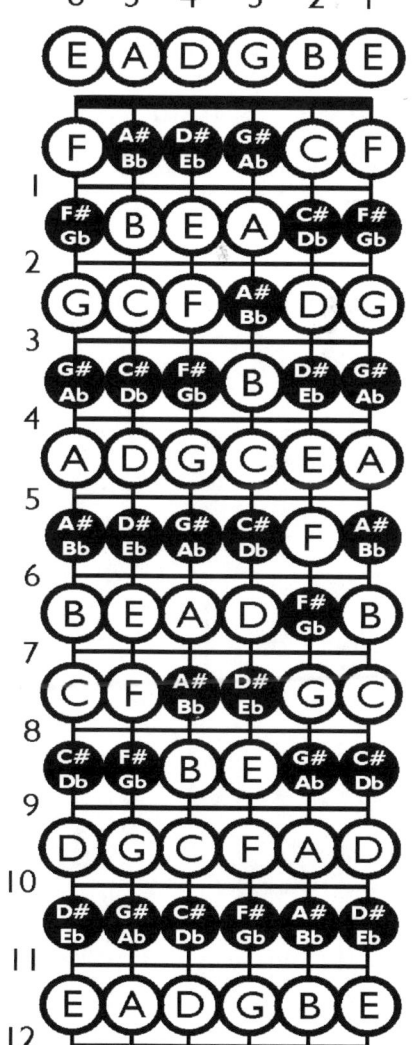

Folksinger 101 Basic Guitar Skills

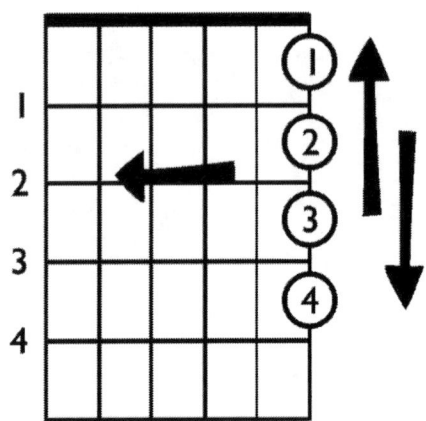

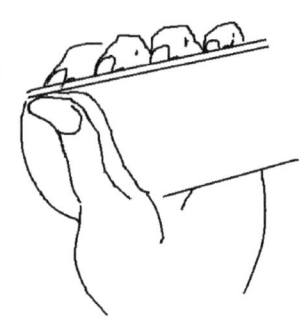

4 Fingers 4 Frets

This is the basic philosophy of good lead guitar and a great exercise for the left hand. Start with the thumb arched back and placed at the center of the neck with the fingers curled and pointed at the fingerboard.

Spreading the fingers apart, strengthening and supporting the 4th finger is critical.

Lean the hand into the curled-up 4th & 3rd fingers. The 1st finger has the capability to stretch back.

Go For a Walk with each pair of fingers stepping up with each finger once on each string. Remember that when you walk one foot is always on the ground while the other is lifting off. Each pair of fingers must be exercised.

Caution!!! If you are 12 years old or younger start at the 7th or 5th frets. Your hand is too small to play any lower on the neck. Small or tight-handed adults can start there as well and work their way down the neck learning to stretch the fingers farther apart as they move to lower frets.

1st to 2nd: Going up! Place the 1st finger at the first fret 6th string and pick that note, place the 2nd finger in front of the 1st at the second fret, pick it and lift off the 1st finger. Place the 1st finger at the first fret 5th string and pick that note, place the 2nd finger in front of the 1st at the second fret, pick it and lift off the 1st finger.

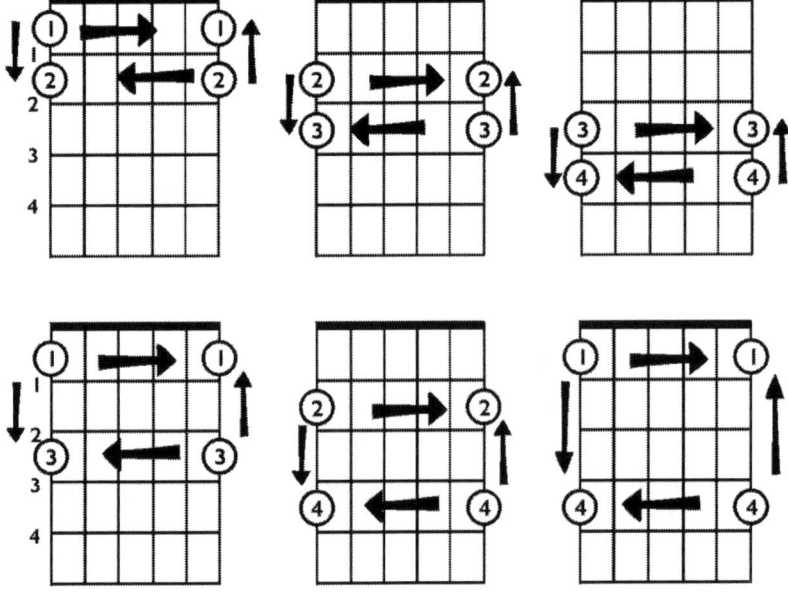

Going Down! Don't forget to lift the second finger and pick the first finger's note.

Pick each note cleanly. Go slow & deliberately.

7

Open C and G7

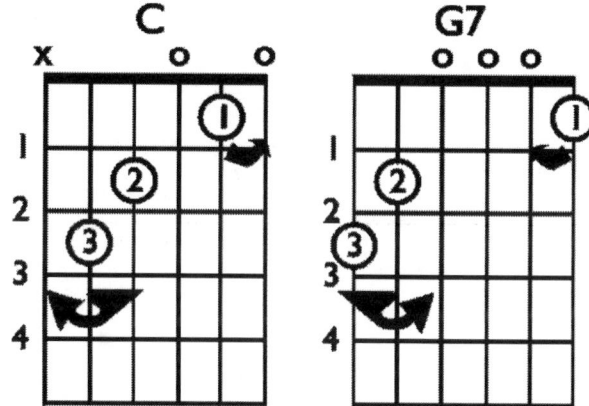

Finger these chords with the third finger first followed by the second and first fingers. The third finger holds the bass note of the chord and gets the highest priority.

Finger hopping C to G7 Change
1) lift the 1st finger
2) hop the 3rd & 2nd fingers to 6th & 5th strings
3) place the 1st finger at the 1st string 1st fret by stretching it back to the note.

The fingers are spread out over 3 frets. Work on each section, splitting the chord into upper and lower movements.
We're hopping a different finger shape from the A and E chords (Slanted instead of vertical). These and all finger shapes are different sounds.

The "Bass Note Rule": the primary bass note of any chord is the lowest note that has the same note name as the chord.

The bass notes are on the 4th, 5th & 6th strings. Land the 3rd finger first on bass notes C for the C chord and G for the G7 because <u>bass notes get highest priority.</u> The bass notes A and E are the open 5th & 6th strings.

Bass Notes & Chord Strums
Bass notes are most often played on beat one with strums following on the remaining beats.
1) Pick the bass note only on beat "one"
2) Strum the higher strings for beats "two, three & four" 4/4-time (1 & 3 total: four beats)

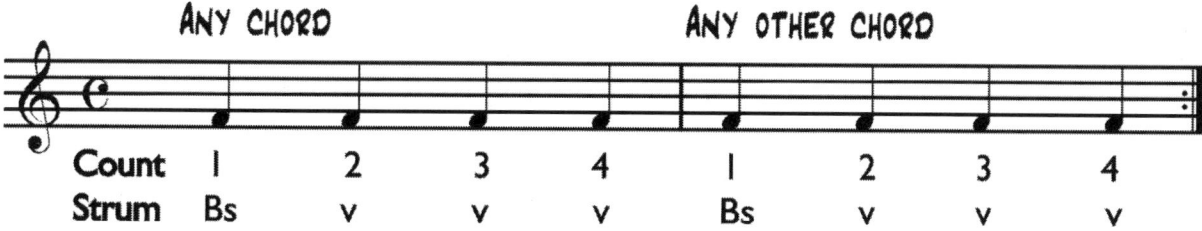

Folksinger 101 Basic Guitar Skills

The Key of C major

This is made of the C major scale and its triad chords. The only key with no flats or sharps. Traditionally, scale steps are numbered with Arabic numerals: 1 -7 and chords are numbered with Roman numerals: **I - VII**. The C major scale is all the plain alphabet notes or white circles on the neck map.

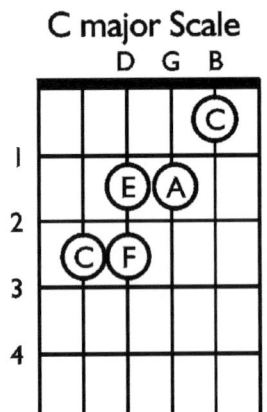
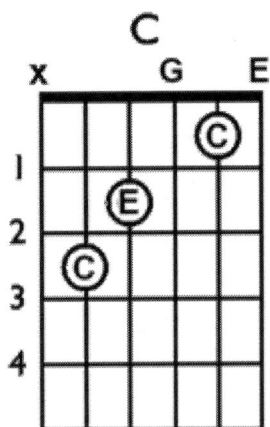

Count the scale! **C1 D2 E3 F4 G5 A6 B7 C8**

Pick each of these notes alphabetically from C up to the higher C and you will hear the familiar "Do re mi" major scale. Play it backwards too. Sing along with note names.

On the staff, notes are individual alphabetical dots like letters. Chords stacks of dots are like words.

Tablature or TAB has six lines for the six strings and numbers for the fret.

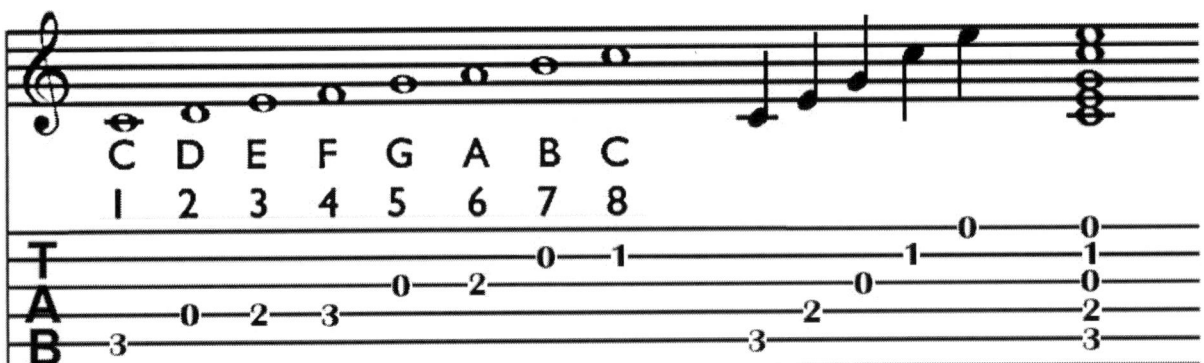

Triads are three note chords, every other note in the scale from the root. Root, 3rd, and 5th C: C E G. When played one note at a time a chord becomes an arpeggio.

3/4 Time "The Waltz"

Just as 4/4 or common time has four quarter notes per bar, a "waltz" is 3/4 and has three quarter notes per bar. Bass note only on "one" and two strums 1+2=3.

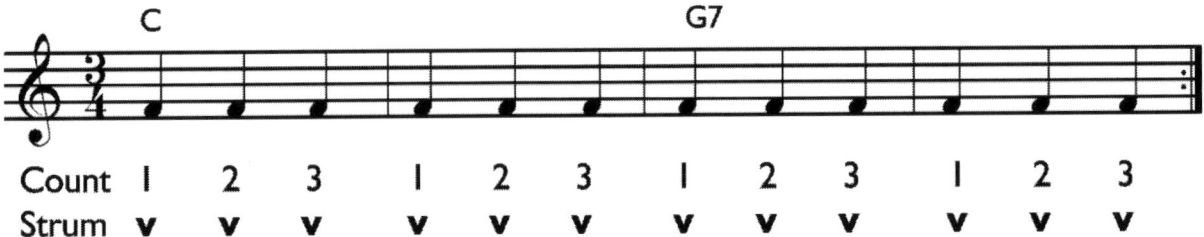

9

Relative Major & Minor:

"Good Guys & Bad Guys" I - VIm

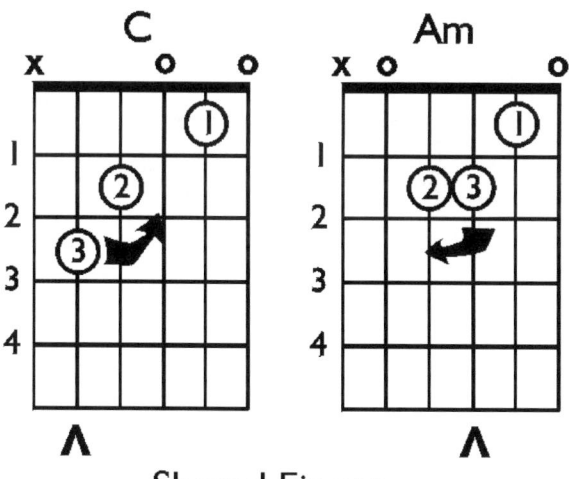

Shared Finger

In the theatre, movies and TV, the musical score will usually reflect the characters. Major keys & chords would be played for the good guys and minor keys & chords for the bad guys.

This major/minor sound is the first element of the psychology of music.

The relative minor is the VI (six) chord counted from the major I (one) chord.

Count on your fingers from one to six, no zeros. C1 D2 E 3 F4 G5 A6
What's the relative minor of G major? Count to six from G.

Shared Fingers

Both the C - Am chord change and the G - Em chord change involves the use of a shared finger with the third finger moving from one side of the second finger to the other.

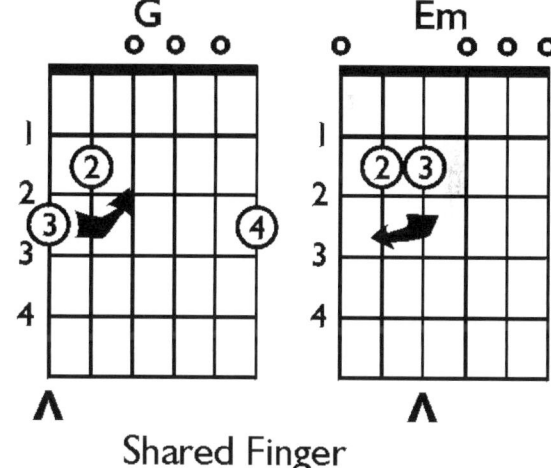

Shared Finger

The Pinky Trick

This G major fingering uses the fourth finger (the Pinky!) and is more versatile than many other fingerings.

Keep the pinky curled up tightly and arched back.

Move the hand to the neck and place the fourth finger on the
1st string while keeping it curled. The second string will work too.
Arch the fingers back at the hand and operate them like little hammers, always landing on the tips. Think of a claw with talons spread.

We use all four fingers of the left hand to play guitar not just three!

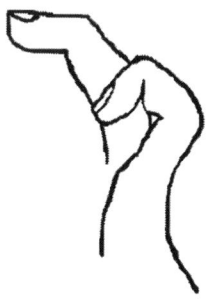

Folksinger 101 Basic Guitar Skills

Two Kinds of A chords: Major and Minor

A Major (A) and A minor (Am) are triad chords which share notes but are NOT in the same key. The C natural note is the minor 3rd and the C# is the major 3rd of A major.

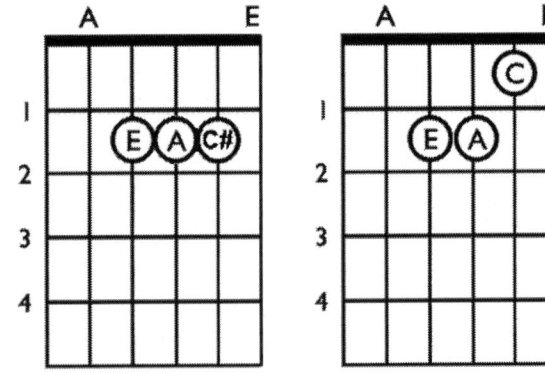

In a chord name, the lower case "m" is the indicator of a minor third.

The note name by itself is assumed to be a major chord.

You will never see the number three in any chord name except when it is "no3rd."

Ano3rd means neither 3rd, C natural or C#, are welcome in the chord, only the root or 1st, A, and the 5th, E. These are the lowest notes of both A and Am. This chord is also known as **A5** and is also called an **open power chord**.

Eighth Notes

Half as long? or twice as fast? Both statements are true. In either case, we are dividing time by 2, cutting each beat into halves.

The eighth note count: 1 and 2 and 3 and 4 and

11

Mixed 1/4 & 1/8 note rhythm.

Most rhythms are mixes of quarter and eighth notes. Try these exercises with your chord changes. Pay attention to the down/up stroke arrows or all down for a rock feel. Pick or Strum down on the numbers, up on the "and".

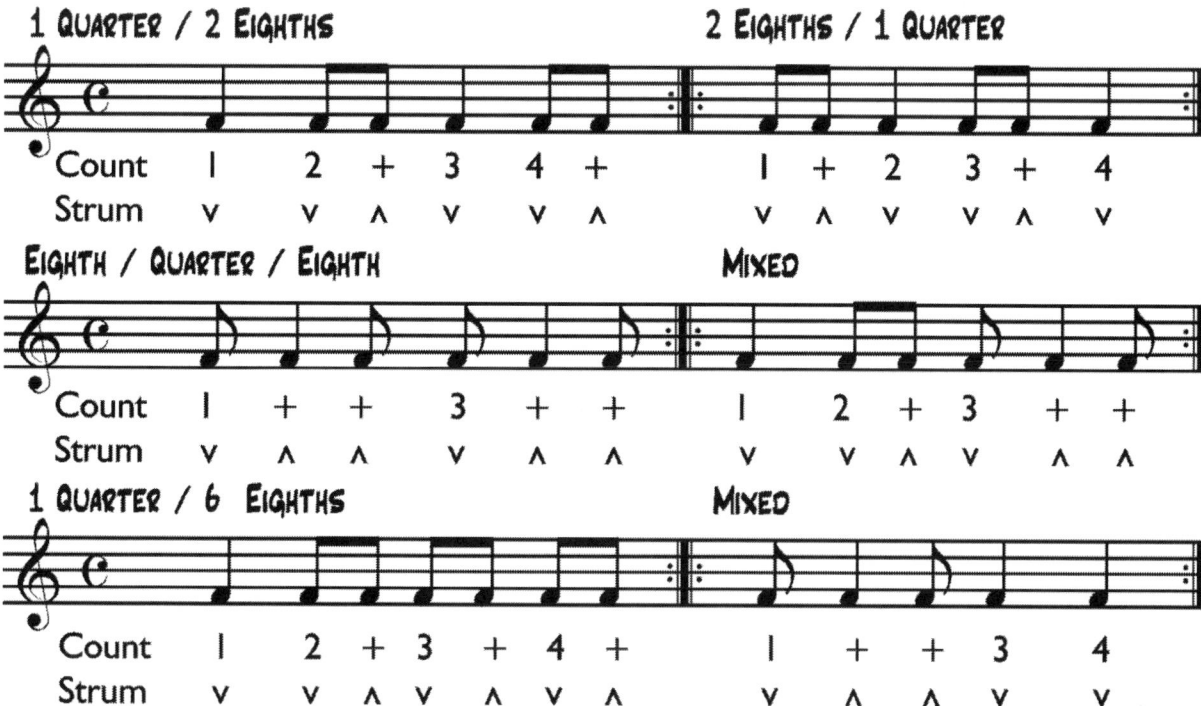

Picking: start with the 1st string, moving the pick only enough to strike the single string. Keep the saying the count as you go. Move to the next lower string and keep the count. Work your way down to the 6th string then come back to the first. Keep it slow and stay accurate. Get a metronome or a drum machine to help keep you steady. Do not rush or drag!

Folksinger 101 Basic Guitar Skills

Guide Fingers

Some chord pairs have a finger that shares the same string at a different fret. The guide finger slides.

A to D
Lift 1st & 2nd fingers.
Slide the 3rd finger up one fret on the 2nd string.
Place 1st & 2nd behind the 3rd finger but split apart on the 3rd and 1st strings.

E to D
Lift 2nd & 3rd fingers.
Slide the 1st finger up one fret.
Place 2nd & 3rd fingers into the corner and on the point of the D triangle.

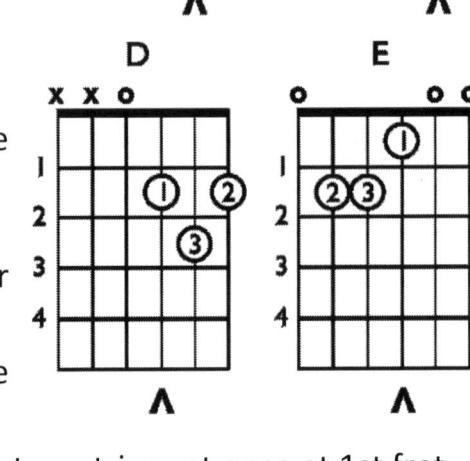

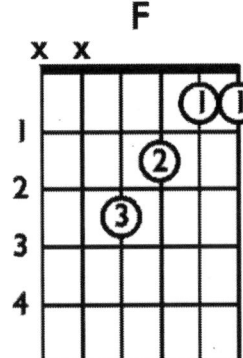

The F Chord is the 1st partial bar chord. Start from a C chord.
Hop the 2nd & 3rd fingers to the middle two strings.
Flop the 1st finger to press down two strings at once at 1st fret.
The third finger bass note is more important than a clear first string.
Fingers should fall over on purpose, never by accident.

Dm or the D minor chord, is the relative minor of F major. Using the 4th finger for the 2nd string is essential to alternate bass notes. Remember that the 2nd finger is a shared finger between F and Dm and should not be lifted.

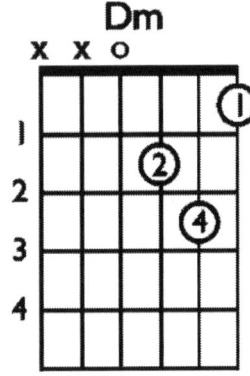

The slash chord is a new kind of chord symbol with an exception to the bass note rule.
The bass note rule makes the lowest D note the bass note of the Dm chord.
Place a backslash and the F note name after the chord symbol, the bass note is changed to the F note while keeping the Dm chord or Dm over F.

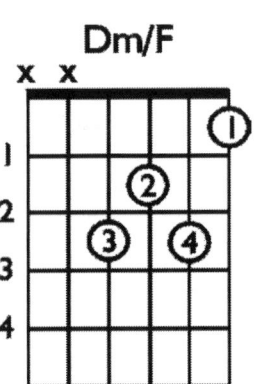

13

Four Fretting Strategies

These strategies are listed from easiest to hardest.
Shared finger is the "if it ain't broke, don't fix it" rule. Just don't move that finger! F to Dm has a shared 2nd finger.

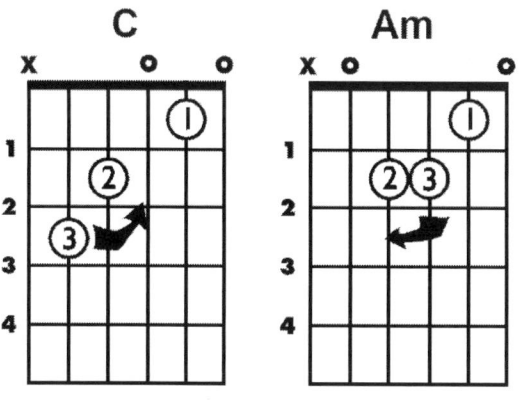

Guide finger is like a shared finger, but it slides keeping contact with the string.

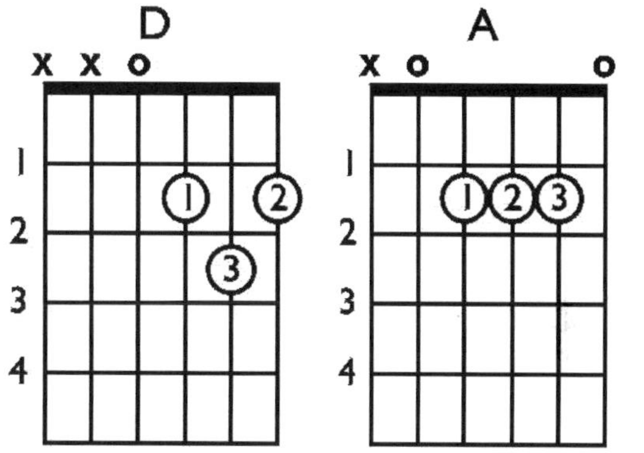

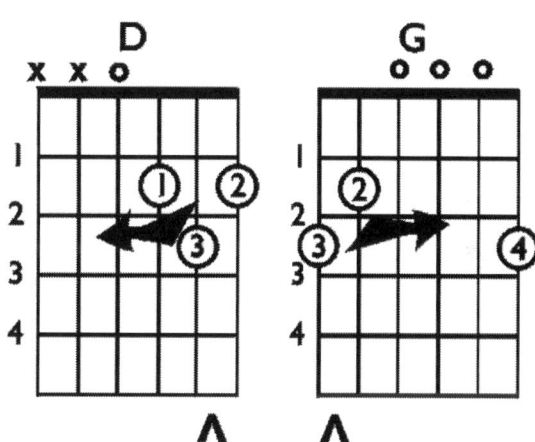

Finger hopping is like flying in formation. D to G and D to C also use this plan.

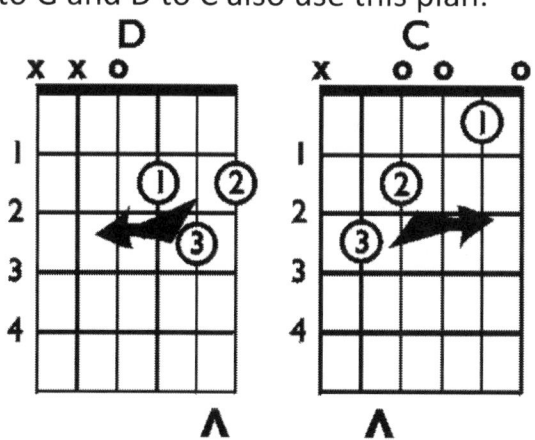

3 & 2 Fingerhop

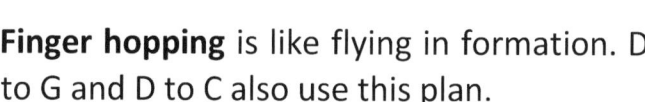

3 & 2 Fingerhop

Follow the leader is the last fretting strategy. If there are no shared fingers, guide finger or finger hopping shapes, we are left with a leader finger. The bass note finger is the leader.

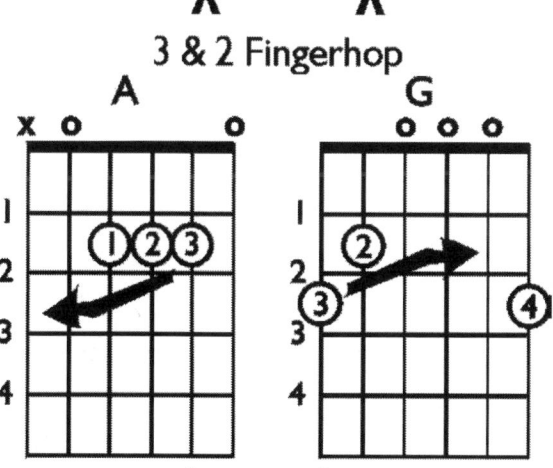

3rd Finger Leader

Three Chord Rock

One Four Five (I - IV – V)

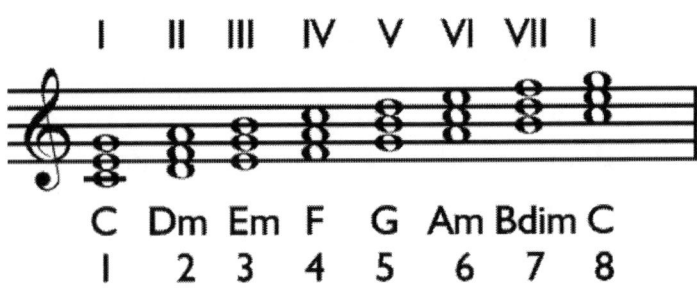

The numerical order of the three most important chords in a major key is one, four and five.

The Mariachi chord order: Primera Segunda Terceira or 1st, 2nd and 3rd are correct order of importance because I to V, tonic to dominant, is much more common than I to IV, tonic to subdominant, or any other chord progression in music.

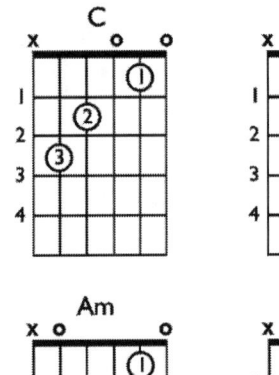
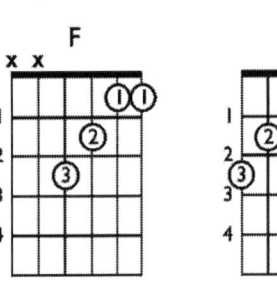
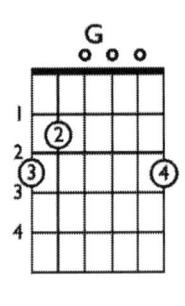
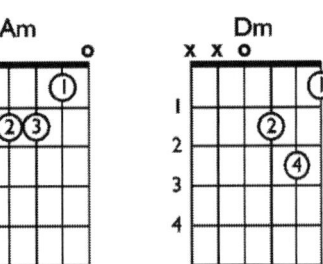
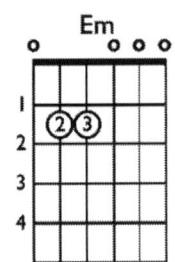

Millions of tunes: classical, country, jazz, rock, and blues use the same two or three chord structure.

The I - IV - V is part of both the harmonized major scale and harmonized minor scale. All major and minor keys are the same.

Let's play "Happy Birthday" with the C, F & G. Start with the C chord, strum it over and over with a basic 3/4 beat.

If you can, sing the first note. The first note is always one of the notes in the background C chord.

Pick the third string, the open G. Start singing the tune from any other note and it will not work. Only one note will work.

At the word "you" the chord changes and you need to figure out which of the two other chords it went to. Is it F or G? From that next chord the new chord change will either return or move on to the third chord.

From F chord the choices are C or G. From G chord the choices are F or C. Other tunes are: "Las Mananitas", "This Land is Your Land", and "Silent Night".

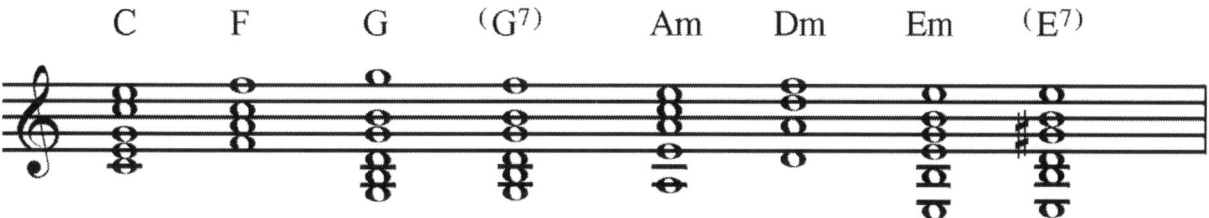

Minor One Four Five (I - IV – V)
How about "La Llorona," "Sinner Man," "Joshua Fought the Battle of Jericho" or "Bad Romance" in Am?

If a minor chord doesn't work perfectly but sounds better than either of the other two chords, try its relative major.

Play Chords by Number 8 Bar Country

People have used this chord progression more than any other for folk and country songs. Like many songs, it is an eight-measure repeating pattern.

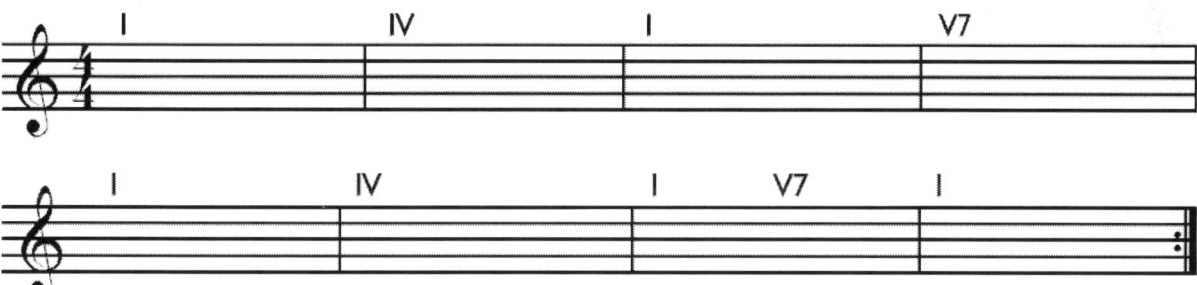

Stock Changes

Like stock footage on TV news, this one-four-five in major and minor system is the normal sound of music. The chords can be mixed in different combinations and timings, usually in two to four chord groups called chord progressions.

Start with the I chord of the key and go to and from every other chord in the harmony of that key. Start again from each chord in the key.

To venture into more adventuresome or weird sounding music we must borrow chords from other keys or change keys.

Folksinger 101 Basic Guitar Skills

V Can Be V7 / Dominant Seventh

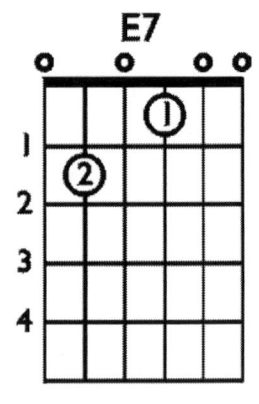

The major and minor chords so far have been triads or three note chords. A common four note chord type are called seventh chords. They are major 7th, minor 7th, dominant 7th and minor 7th flat 5. Of these seventh chords, only the dominant 7th, gets used with triads often. The only "normal" dominant 7 is the fifth chord of the major or minor harmony: the "V7".

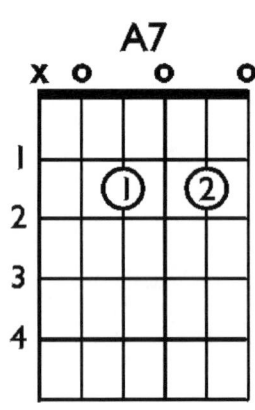

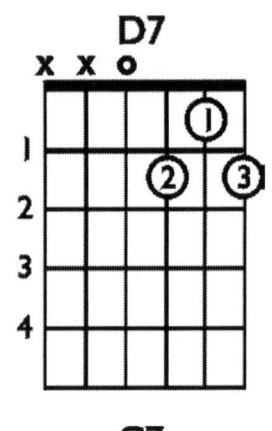

E7 leads to A or Am,
A7 leads to D or Dm,
D7 leads to G or Gm,
G7 leads to C or Cm,
C7 leads to F or Fm,
B7 leads to E or Em,

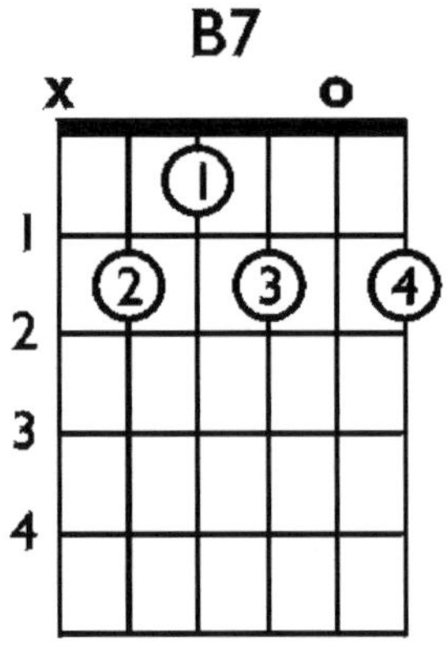

C major I-IV-V is C, F and G7.
A minor I-IV-V is Am, Dm and E7.

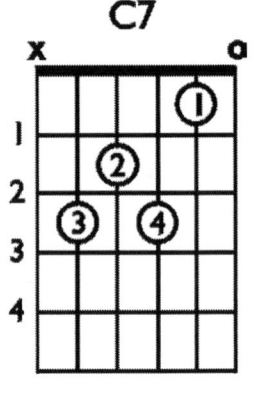

Dominant Seventh and the Blues

What if the three chords turned into Dominant seventh chords? You get the Blues!

I7 - IV7 - V7 Chord progressions "dominate" the Blues and Early Rock & Roll. One progression, the 12 Bar Blues, is used in all American music.

1) Memorize the I-IV-V chords
2) Convert All chords to "7" chords.
3) Play the Blues (Rock Around the Clock by Bill Haley and the Comets, Hound Dog by Elvis, Johnny B Goode by Chuck Berry, Workin' Man's Blues by Merle Haggard, Red House by Jimi Hendrix, Crossroads by Robert Johnson/Eric Clapton, Rock and Roll by Led Zepplin, and many more).

12 Bar Blues

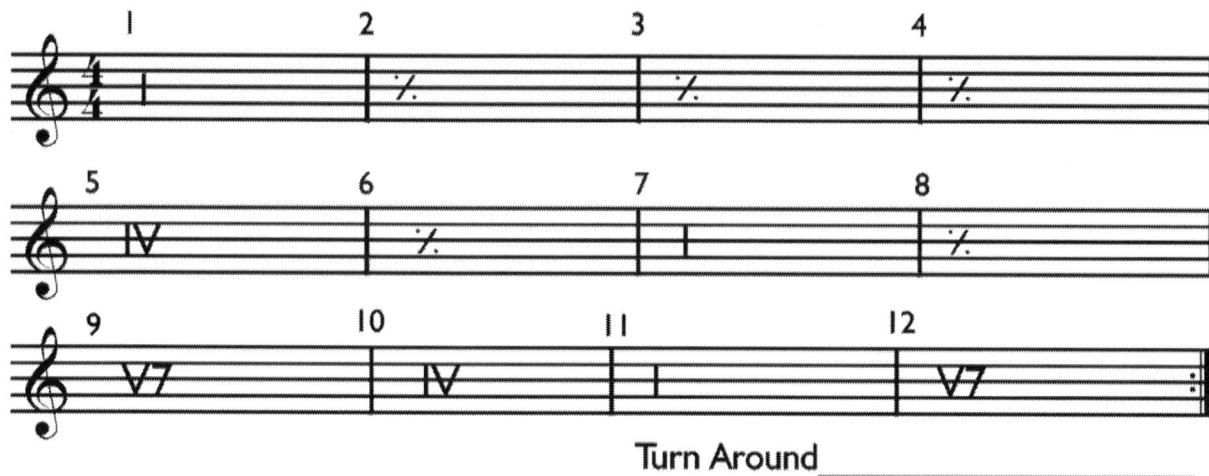

Triplets & Compound Meter

In 4/4 time, triplets are indicated by the "3" over or under the group of three notes. This is called a "triplet sign" and squeezes three notes into the time normally reserved for two (eighth notes).

Triplets can be fixed as the normal division of rhythm with compound meters such as 6/8 & 12/8. These "Time Sigs" have a "Main Pulse" at beat 1, 4, 7, and 10.
All rhythms are based on Groupings (aka Time Sigs) and Divisions (1/8 notes, triplets & more!). Eighth Notes Rock. Triplets Roll.

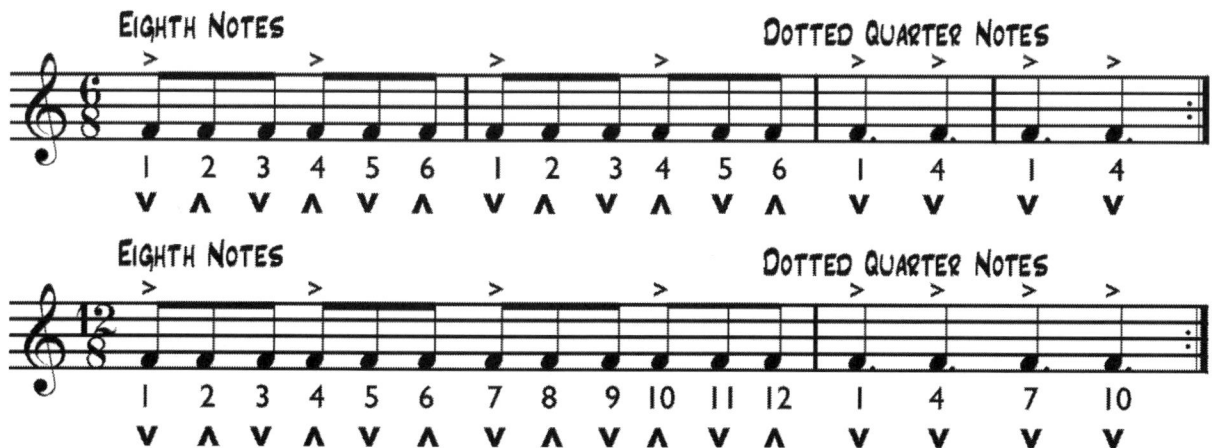

First Review

Asking the right questions is very important to gaining a truly complete understanding. Here are a few basic ones.

What is the neck of the guitar?
Where is the body of the guitar?
Where is the nut? What are frets? Where is the bridge?
How many strings does the guitar have?
What is tuning a guitar about?
How is the guitar tuned by ear?
What are the names and numbers of the open strings?
What is finger hopping?
What is common time? How is it counted?
What is 4/4 time? How is it counted?
What is the musical alphabet?
What is a sharp and what does it do?
What is a flat and what does it do?
What are the natural half steps?
What are the notes in the C major scale?
How many notes are in a triad chord?
What is the "go for a walk" exercise?
How does the neck map work?
What is 3/4 time? How is it counted?
What is the bass note of a C chord?
Which beat number is the bass note usually played on?
What is the relative minor chord and which chord number does it get? eg: 1 is C
What are shared fingers?
What are eighth notes and how are they counted?
What are guide fingers?
What is three chord rock and what are the numbers?
Which of the three chords can also become a dominant seventh chord?
How many measures are in the 12-bar blues?
What are triplets? How do you count them?

The Musical Staff

Lines and Spaces - 2 Sayings

There are a couple of traditional sayings used to help memorize the lines and spaces of the treble clef and staff: Every Good Boy Does Fine and FACE. But I prefer the funnier sayings:

Elvis' Guitar Broke Down Friday

Fat Alley Cats Eat Garbage

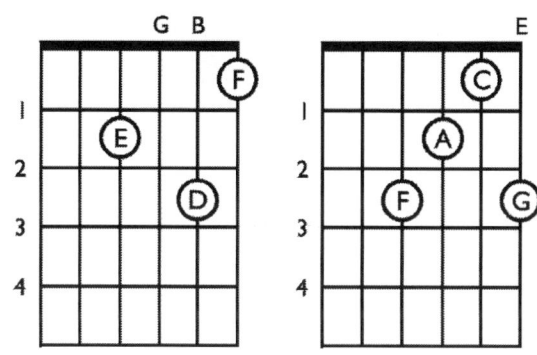

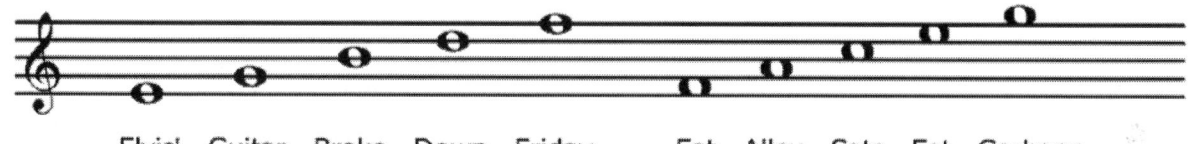

The note names are arranged in alphabetical order, Line to Space to Line, going up the staff and reverse order, of course, coming down the staff.

Note heads get placed either "In the Space", not crossing the lines on either side or "On the Line", centered on the line and not touching the lines on either side. Stems go up on the right if the note head is below the middle line and down on the left if it is above. Note on and off or note and rest values are based on the beat counting and division we've discussed before. 4/4 time works like fractions of an inch.

Folksinger 101 Basic Guitar Skills

Notes on the 1st and 2nd String.

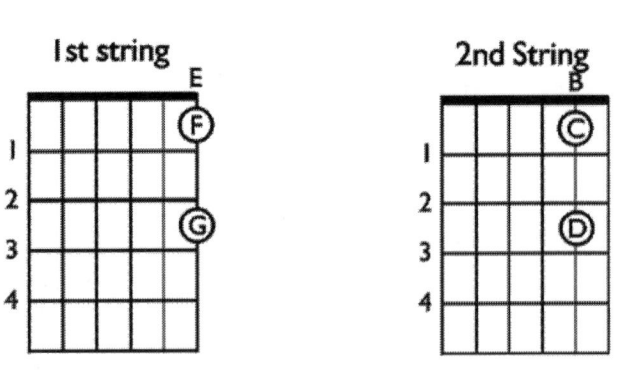

The 1st String open is the E as in "Eat", the 1st string 1st fret is the F as in "Friday" and the 1st string 3rd fret is the G as in "Garbage."

The 2nd String open is the B as in "Broke", the 2nd string 1st fret is the C as in "Cats" and the 2nd string 3rd fret is the D as in "Down".

Eat Friday Garbage Broke Cats Down

Finger Seating: Keep the 1st finger at the first fret while pressing the 3rd finger at the third fret.

Lazy Guitarist Credo: "If I don't need to lift a finger... I won't".

Mystery Tune! Copy the notes, work up the tab and play this tune.

21

Yet Another Mystery Tune

Flats, Sharps & Naturals

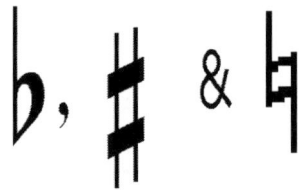

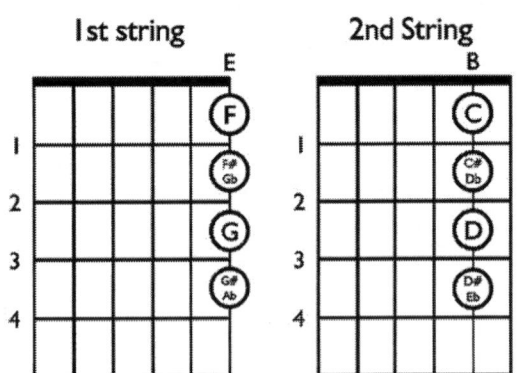

The note map has white circles for the natural notes and black circles for the accidentals: flats & sharps.

A flat makes a note one half step lower than normal pitch and a sharp makes a note one half step higher than normal.

A natural is a sharp or flat fixer! A reset!

An open string can be sharped but cannot be flatted. Eb cannot be on the E string.

E   F   F#/Gb   G   G#/Ab   B   C   C#/Db   D   D#/Eb

Every other key than C/Am uses at least one flat or sharp. The key of G/Em uses F# or the raised 7th and the key of F/Dm uses Bb or a lower 4th.

They can indicate a key signature: one or more sharps or flats after the clef.

KEY OF C   KEY OF G   KEY OF C   KEY OF F
E F G   E F# G   D C B   D C Bb

They can also be added on a note-by-note basis and after a double bar line to indicate a key change. Draw a few examples for yourself.

Sing all music notation examples by note name to train the eyes and ears. Men will need to sing an octave lower.

Dots & Ties

Ties are rhythmic glue. Tying a half note to a quarter note makes a three-beat long note. 2+1=3. Dotting a half note also makes it three beats long. Dots add half of the value of the note it is attached to. 2+1=3. Count along as you play each example.

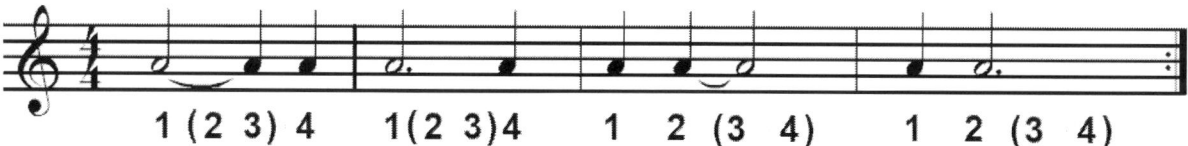
1 (2 3) 4   1(2 3)4   1 2 (3 4)   1 2 (3 4)

Hit beat one and hold, then hit beat four. Or hit beat one and two and hold to the next beat one.

Tying a quarter note to an eighth note makes it worth one and a half beats. Dotting the quarter note also makes it worth one and a half beats.

1   (2) +   3 (4) +   1 + (2)   3 +   (4)

Hit beat one and hold past beat two and hit the "and" of two then three. Say: One, (two) and three.

Dots work only within the measure. Ties can cross the bar lines. The number of beats tied is calculated by basic addition. This is a very popular beat! The "and" of beat two is tied to beat three, then the "and" of three is struck leading into beat four. This is called "syncopation". We emphasize the off beats!

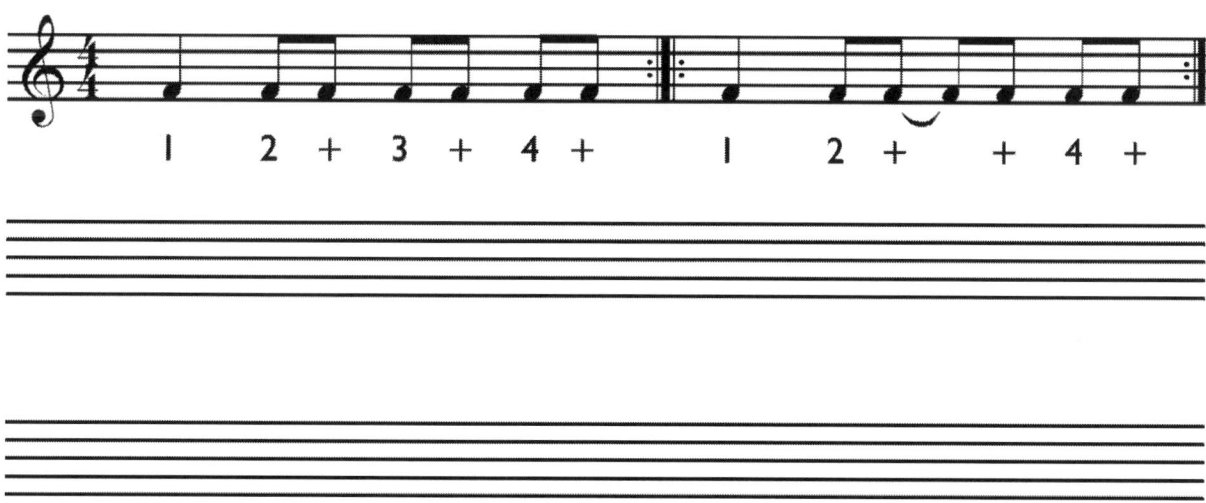
1   2 + 3 + 4 +   1   2 +   + 4 +

Folksinger 101 Basic Guitar Skills

Notes on the 3rd & 4th Strings

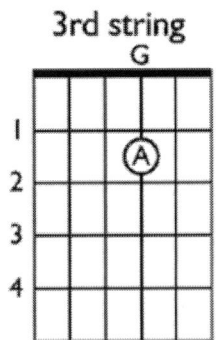
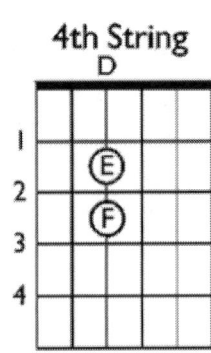

The 3rd string has two natural notes: "G" & "A". "Guitar Alley".

The 4th string is your highest bass string and has three natural notes: "D ", "E " & "F." Bass notes: "Dead Elvis Fat."

Remember to keep your fingertips down, near the fret and your knuckles arched and spread apart. Sing all notes by name. Girl may need to sing an octave higher.

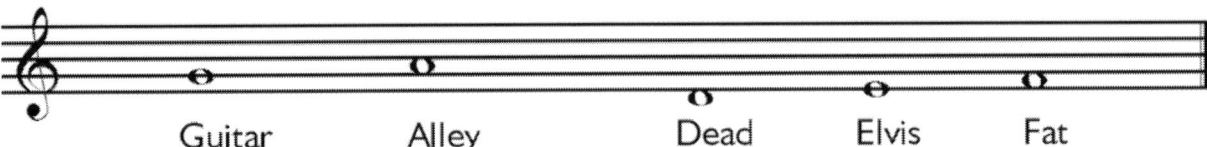

More Flats & Sharps

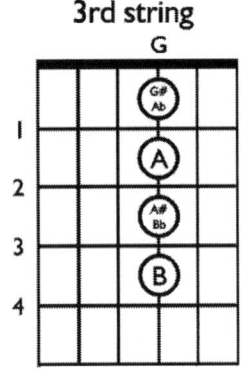
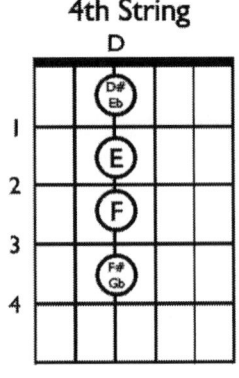

The 3rd string first fret is G#/Ab, the 3rd string 3rd fret is the A#/Bb, and the 3rd string 4th fret is a duplicate B (same as open 2nd string) The 4th string 1st fret is D#/Eb. The 4th string 4th fret is F#/Gb. F# is in every key with sharps and is the most popular sharp of all.

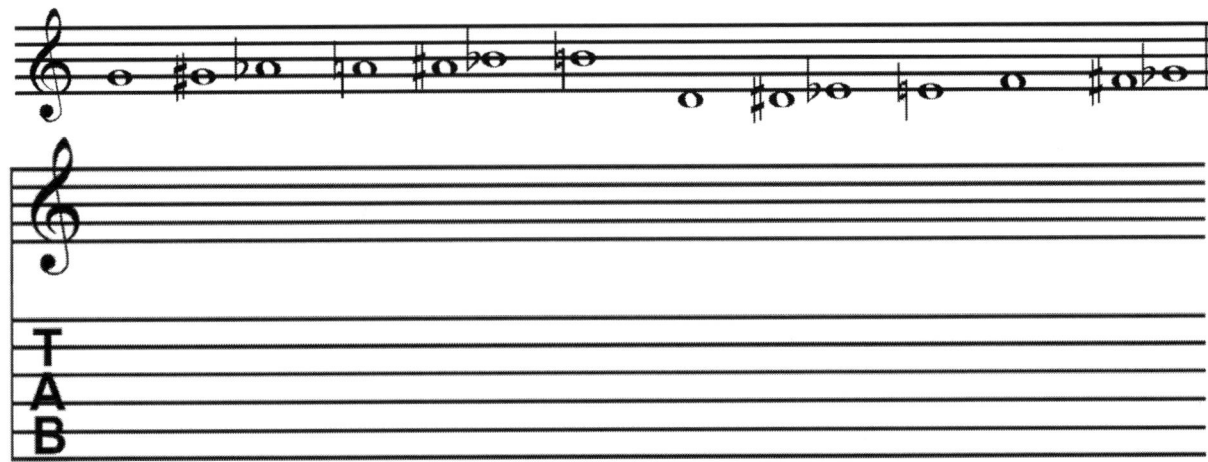

More Mystery Tunes

This tune uses a half beat "pick up note" whose count is the "and of two" and leads into beat "one". The time is stolen from the last bar of the tune.

These tunes all have a new key signature: F# for the key of G/Em. It means that every "F" is sharp. Here's a tune in the key of Em.

Folksinger 101 Basic Guitar Skills

Notes on the 5th & 6th Strings

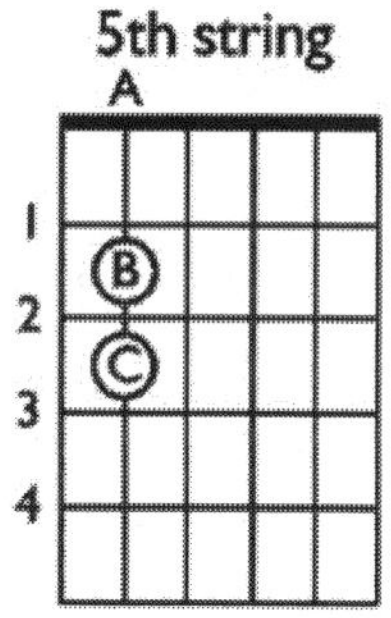

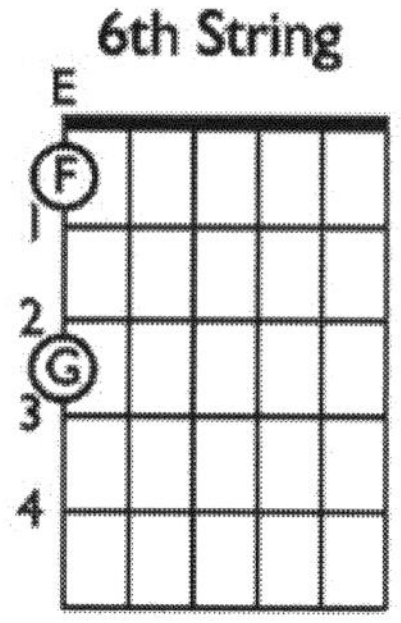

5th string — A: B at 2nd fret, C at 3rd fret.

6th String — E: F at 1st fret, G at 3rd fret.

These are the very lowest bass notes on the guitar.

The 5th string has the natural notes: A, B at the 2nd fret and C at the 3rd fret.

The 6th String has natural notes: E, F at the 1st fret and G at the 3rd fret.

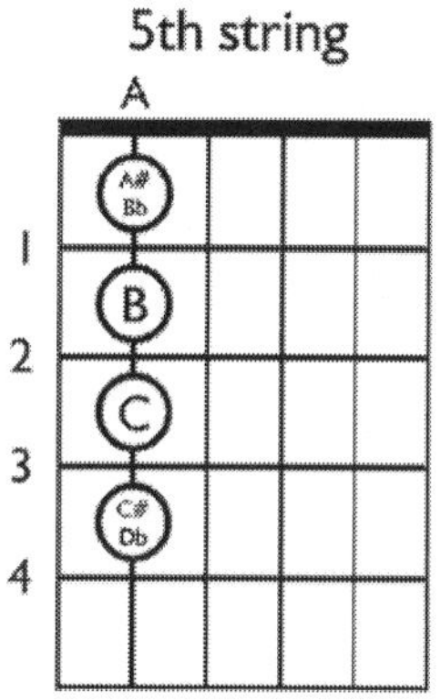

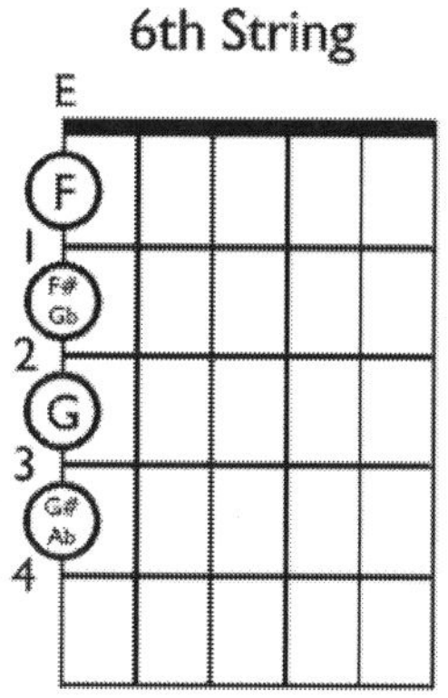

Notes shown on staff: A B C E F G

Count the Ledger Lines

Three lines down is F, hanging from it is E. Two lines down is A, hanging from it is G. One line down is C, hanging from it is B. Counting ledger lines is the quickest way to read ledger lines.

Singing will become difficult as we get lower. The low E note is below the vocal range of all women and most men.

Notes shown with accidentals: A A#/Bb B C C#/Db E F F#/Gb G G#/Ab

Little pieces of the highest lines of bass clef, A and F, become the ledger lines in treble clef. Middle C is in the middle. Bass clef staff which has lines and spaces like treble clef but shifted one line lower.

Good Burritos Don't Fall Apart   All Cows Eat Grass

Folksinger 101 Basic Guitar Skills

Even More Mystery Tunes!

Bass Lines

Music is full of bass lines moving from root to fifth. The root is the primary bass note. The fifth is the secondary bass note. The chord name of C can change to C/G or "C over G".

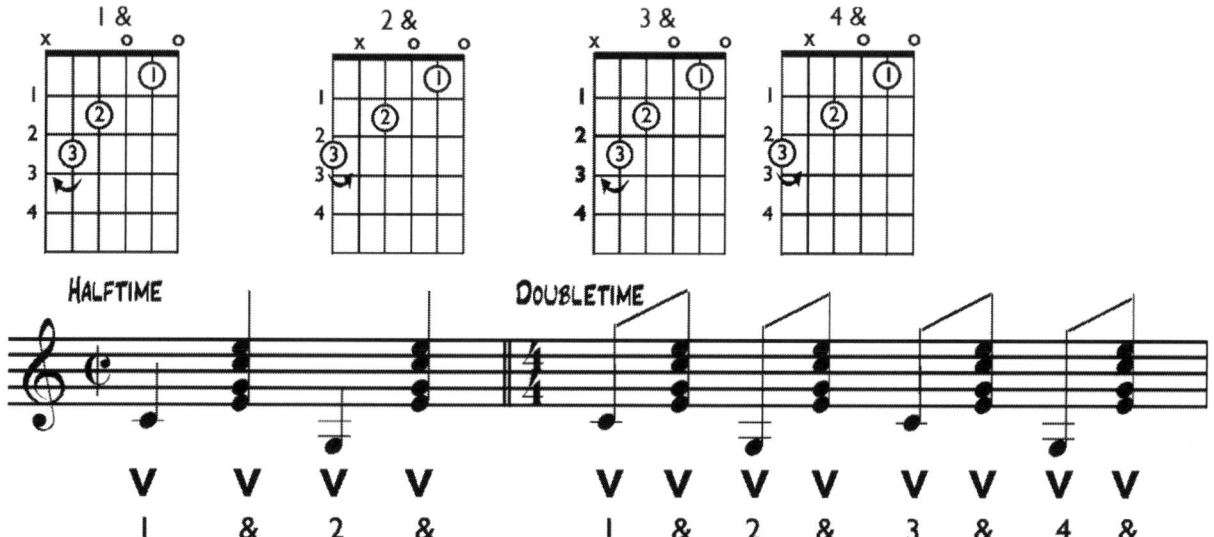

Pick the primary bass note and strum the upper part of the chord then pick the secondary bass note and strum the upper part of the chord again.

CUT TIME: a C with a line slicing through it vertically. This indicates a 2/2 count instead of a 4/4 count. It means quarter note get counted like eighth notes.

Walk Up and Walk Down Bass Line

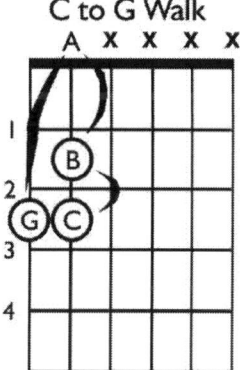

This bass line uses a standard walk up the scale to the next root when changing chords. When moving from the G to a C chord the first two quarter notes are a G bass note and an upper chord strum. The last two quarter notes are a climb from note A to B to the C bass note and chord.

When moving from the C down to an G chord the first two quarter notes are a C bass note and an upper chord strum. The last two quarter notes are bass note B to A to the G bass note on beat one.

Folksinger 101 Basic Guitar Skills

The Major Minor Yin Yang

The pairing of a major key with a minor key is a cliché' as old as black & white or good and evil. These sounds have been used for centuries to indicate to audiences exactly those moods and qualities.

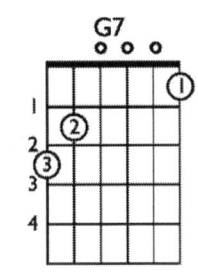

Six is the bad guy's number and three is the good guy's number. C1 D2 E3 F4 G5 A6 and A1 B2 C3.

The relative minor **VIm** chord of a major key becomes the **Im** of the minor key.
The relative major **III** chord of the minor key becomes the **I** of the major key.
The major key has three major chords in a one-four-five pattern.
The minor key has three minor chords in a one-four-five pattern.
Both **V** chords can be dominant seventh **V7**.

Both major and minor keys have the same basic **I-IV-V** structure but the other chords: II, III, VI and VII are different in major and minor.

In a major key, the II, III and VI are minor chords and VII is a half-diminished or minor seven flat five chord.

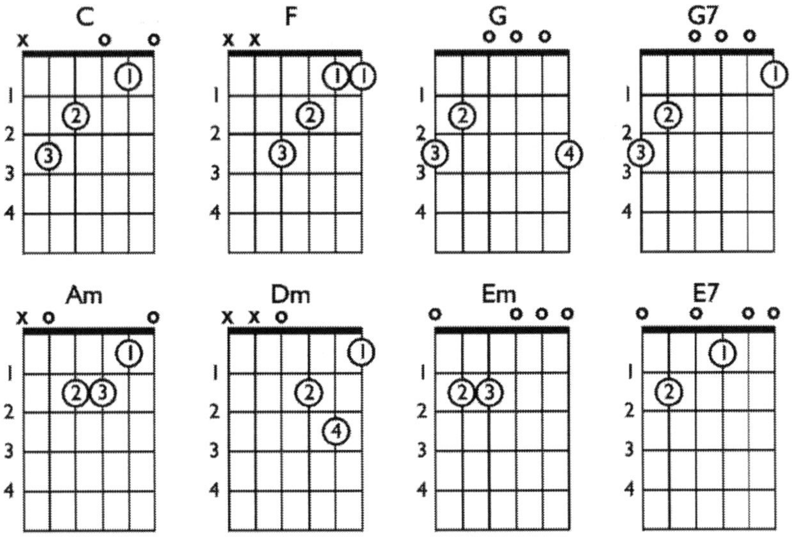

In a minor key, II is the m7b5 (half-diminished chord) and III, VI and VII are major chords.

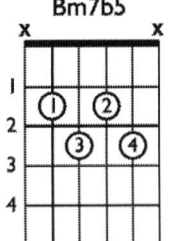
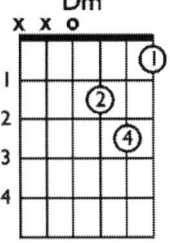
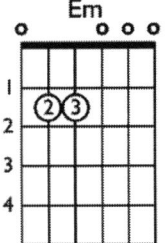
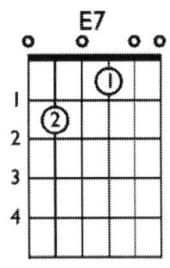

Changing the Key is the solution to the complaint "It is too high!" or too low. Every note is moved the same distance. In this case it moves a 4th lower from C to G.

Jingle Bells starts on the 3rd of the key of C so it must begin on the 3rd of the key of G: B.

Chord Numbers

Chords are numbered within a key.

Major key 1 4 1 5 - C: C F C G7

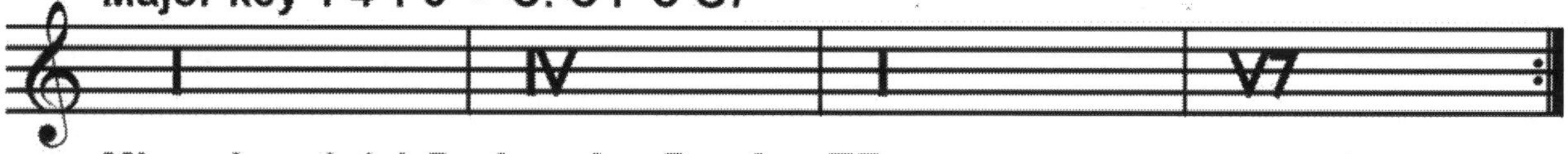

I
IV
I
V7

Minor key 1 4 1 5 - Am: Am Dm Am E7

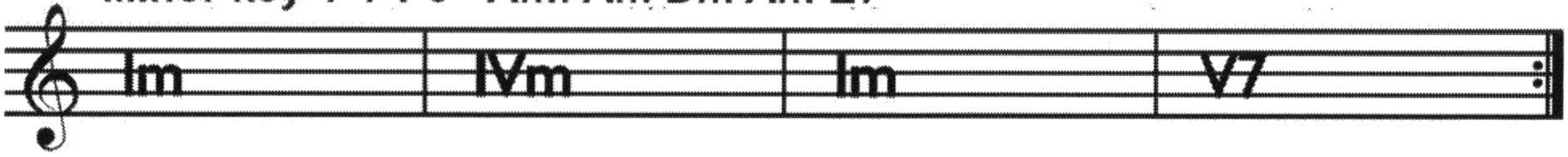

Im
IVm
Im
V7

Major key 1 6 2 5 the oldies - C: C Am Dm G7

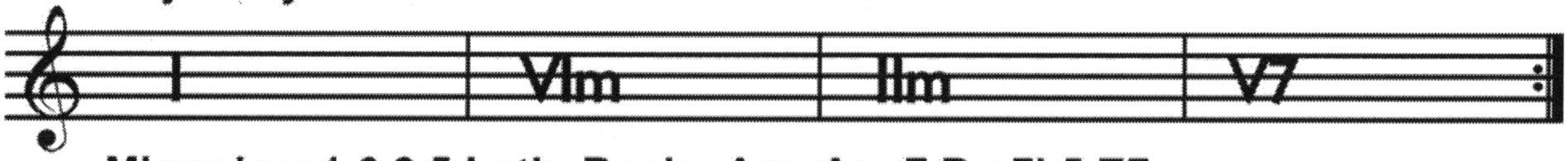

I
VIm
IIm
V7

Minor key 1 6 2 5 Latin Rock - Am: Am F Bm7b5 E7

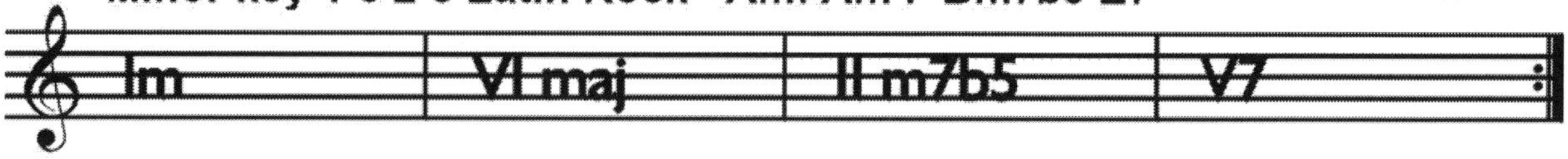

Im
VI maj
II m7b5
V7

Major key 1 2 3 4 Climb C: C Dm Em F

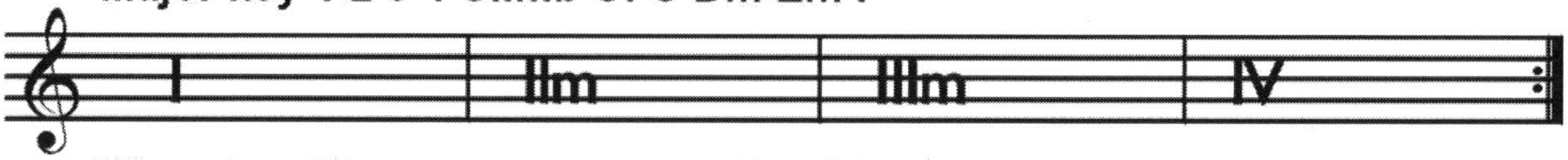

I
IIm
IIIm
IV

Minor key Flamenco Drop Am: Am G F E7

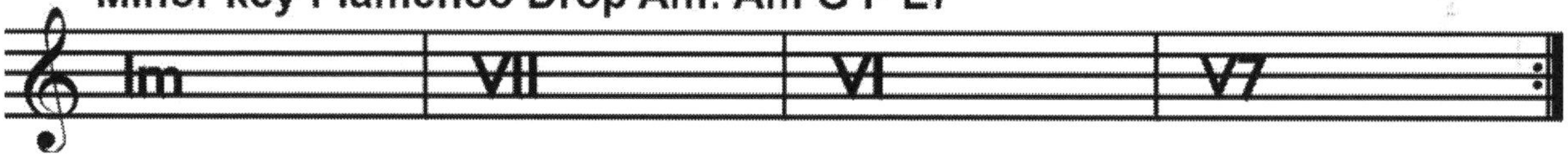

Im
VII
VI
V7

Changing the Key with Capos

F
F/C
F bar chord
1
2
3
4

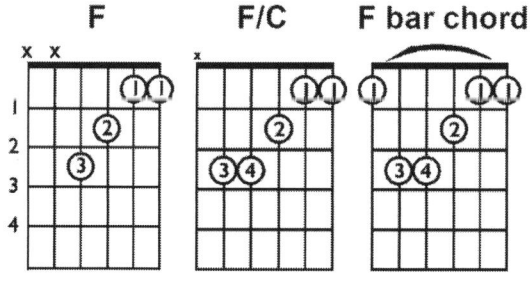

On the neck map at each intersection a note lives! The ultimate key change device: the CAPO! It works like a fake finger.

A capo allows basic open chords to work in any key. The capo raises the pitch of each string to the pitch at the fret it is clamped behind. When you place the capo across the strings at the first fret the 5th string note changes from an "A" to a "Bb" and the A chord becomes a Bb chord.

Bb
Bb
CAPO

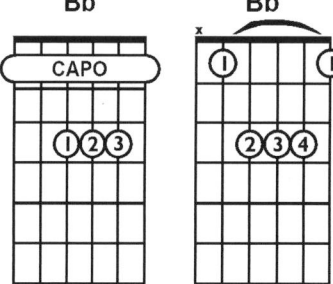

Folksinger 101 Basic Guitar Skills

E string is F, the A is Bb, the D is Eb, G is Ab, C is Db and F is Gb or F#.

If you move the capo to the 2nd fret the bass note on the 6th string becomes F# and now the A note is a B and Am becomes Bm.

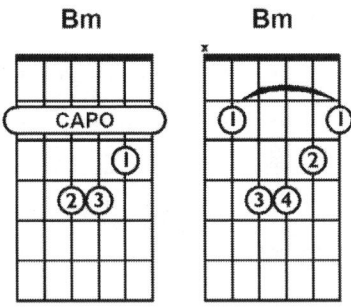

1st or 2nd fret capo makes the key one note higher.

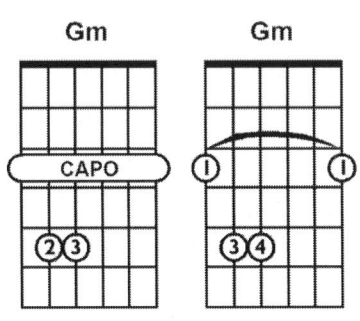

Capo at the 3rd fret and it becomes the key of C major. At the 3rd or 4th fret moves the key two steps up.

Key of A chords (A, D and E7) are now key of C chords (C, F and G7). E major and Em are now G major and Gm because the 6th string "E" is now "G".

Cheap Tricks

Chord names have numbers in them to alter the sound. Simple moves on the guitar can make great sounds. Have a few D Tricks.

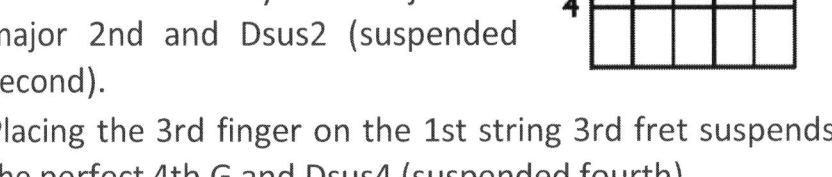

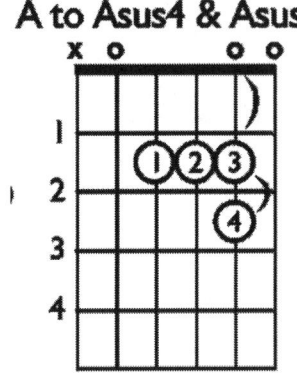

Lift the 2nd finger from the 1st string and expose the open E note. E is the 2nd note in the key of D major: the major 2nd and Dsus2 (suspended second).

Placing the 3rd finger on the 1st string 3rd fret suspends the perfect 4th G and Dsus4 (suspended fourth).

"Cheap Tricks" for A major

Lift the 3rd finger from the 2nd string opening the B note, the major 2nd, to make Asus2. Place the 4th finger on the 3rd fret 2nd string for the perfect 4th D and the Asus4.

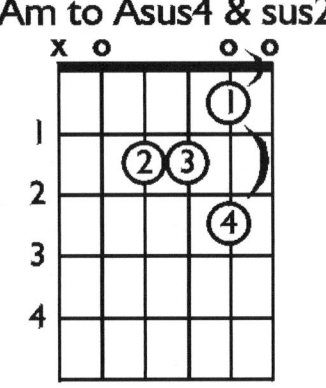

What About Am?

The same B and D notes are 2nd and 4th. The sound resolves to the major 3rd C# in the key of A major and the minor 3rd C in the key of A minor. The third of "A" <u>must</u> be "C" <u>something,</u> natural, flat, or sharp! It <u>cannot</u> be a "B" or "D" because they are 2nd and 4th in the key.

The Hammer On & the Pull Off A "Hammer On" is landing the finger very hard on the string behind the fret. A "Pull Off" is plucking the string with a finger of the left hand.

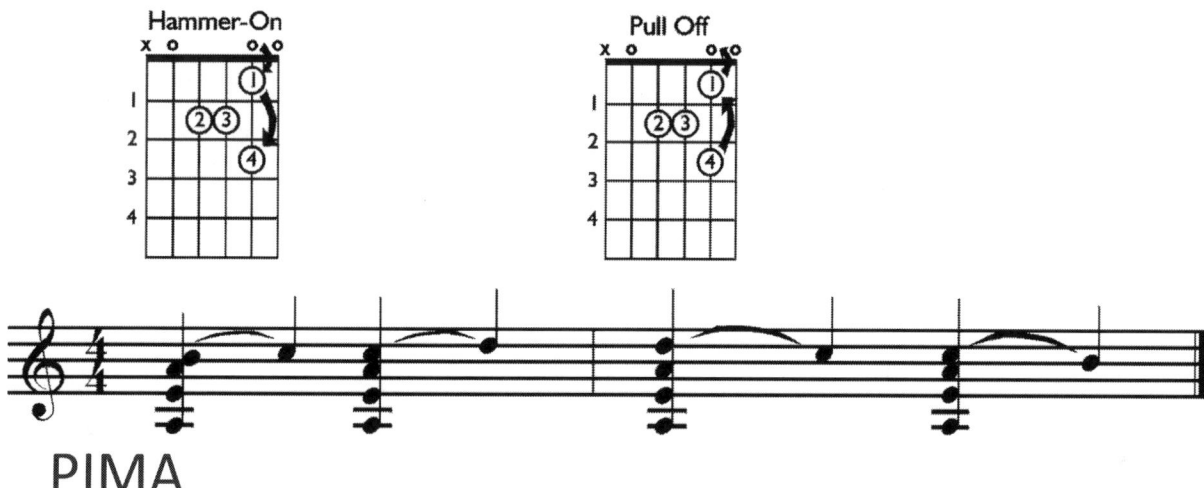

PIMA

The Classical Guitar system of PIMA is my preference due to the great number of pieces written for Classical Guitar with these fingerings. **PIMA: Pulgar, Indice, Medio y Anular.**

Pick a bass note with the side of your thumb then pick across each of the three higher strings with each of the fingers.

Right Hand Fingers:	Thumb	Index	Middle	Ring
Folk Fingerstyle:	T	I	M	R
Classical Guitar:	P	I	M	A

Pinch them all together and in thumb and single finger pairs.

Besides playing chord arpeggios, the fingers can play scale lines by using alternating fingers: imim is the favorite but we also use mimi, mama, amam, ami, ima. Any possible combination can be seen.

Free Strokes: Pluck the string with a fingertip and stay in the air. Do not touch the next string.

Rest Strokes: Play the first string and rest the fingertip on the second string after plucking the first.

Pulgar strikes the string with the side of the finger, not the tip, in a circular motion. Keep the thumb in front of the fingers not behind.

Folksinger 101 Basic Guitar Skills

Classical Guitar is one of the most complete ways to play a guitar with bass lines melody and chord all happening at once. There is also a collection of wonderful music dating back hundreds of years. It is the most technically demanding guitar style.

Travis Picking (outside-inside roll)

This classic bluegrass pattern uses opposing thumb / finger movement and can become quite speedy. Thanks to the late great Merle Travis of Tennessee.

Open Power Chords & The Blues

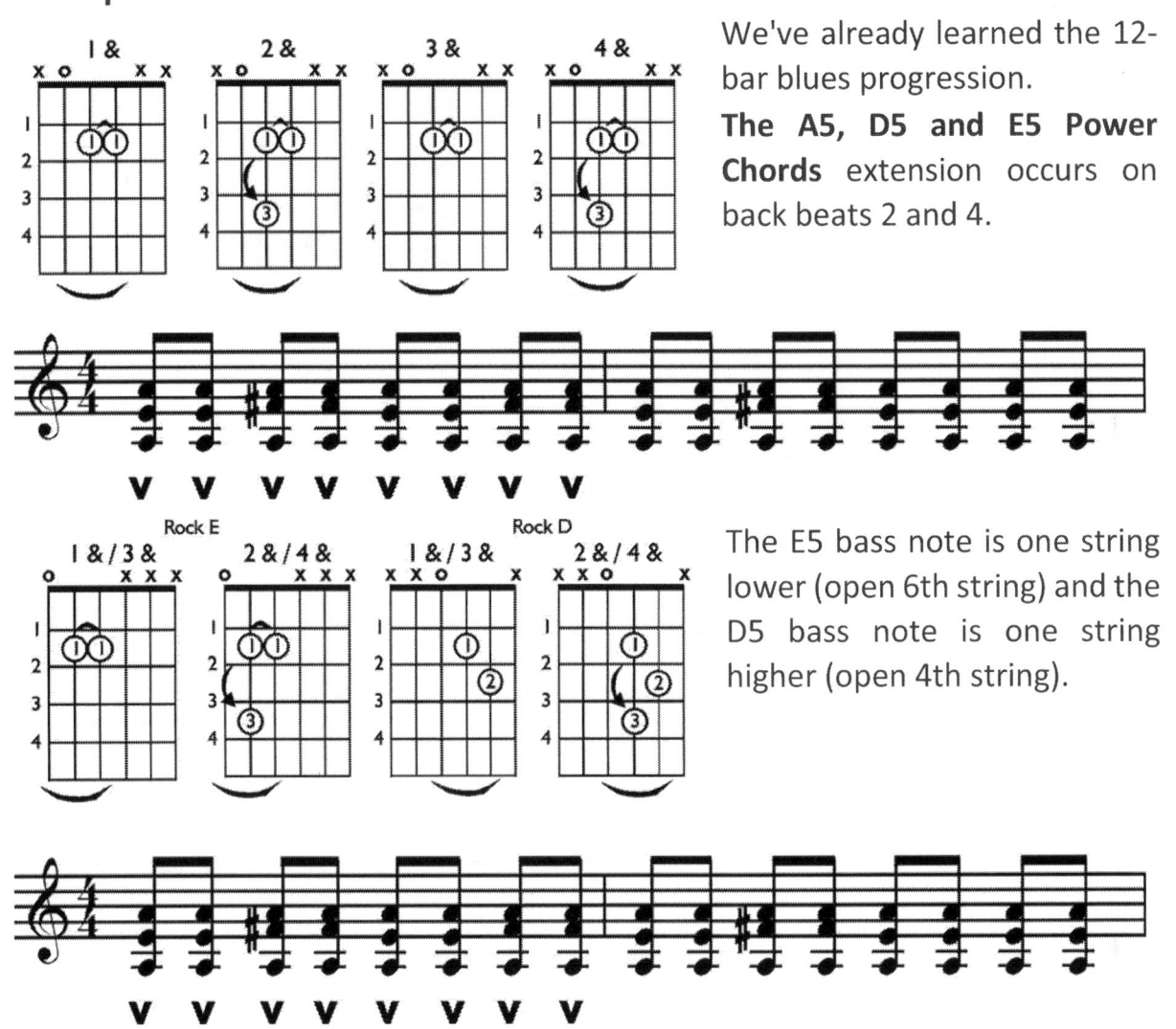

We've already learned the 12-bar blues progression.

The A5, D5 and E5 Power Chords extension occurs on back beats 2 and 4.

The E5 bass note is one string lower (open 6th string) and the D5 bass note is one string higher (open 4th string).

The 8 Bar Blues Progression

This 8-bar blues is a seldom used but neat chord progression. Related to the 8 bar country changes & 12 bar blues, these "changes" are used in traditional gospel Music.

12 Bar Quick Change Blues

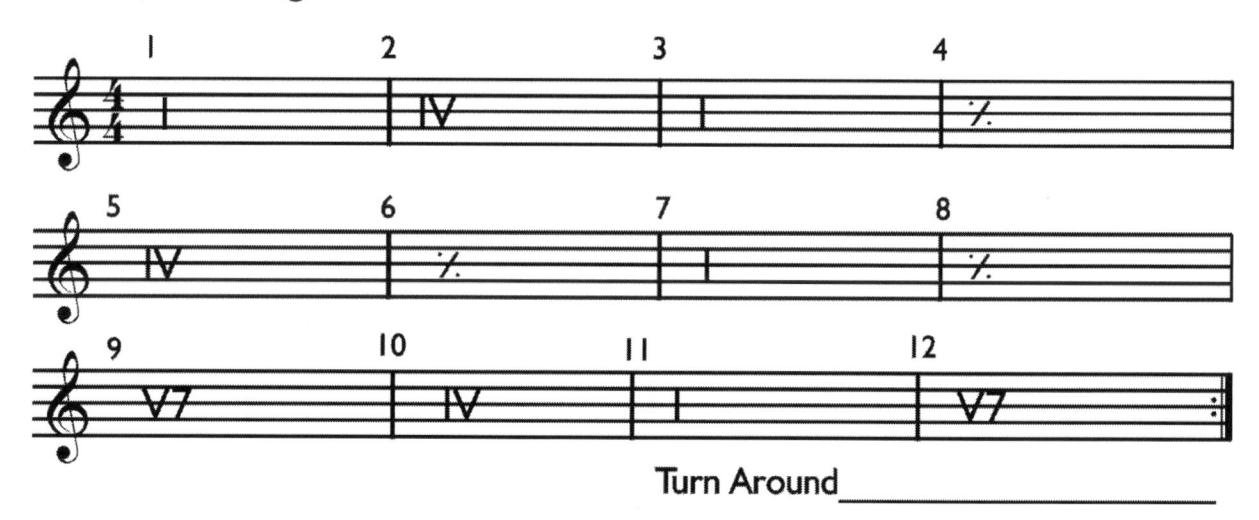

The Shuffle and Swing

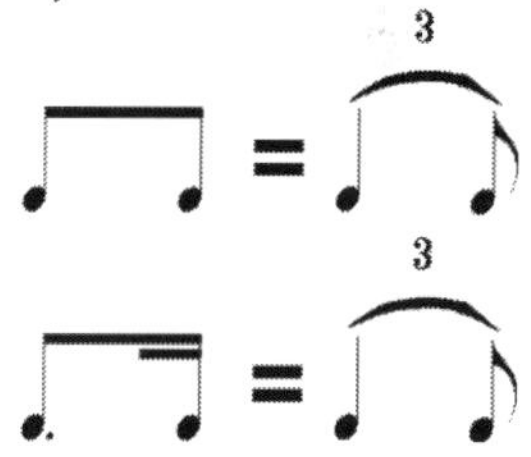

Triplets without the "trip" is the best way of describing basic "Swing". This fascinating rhythm is the heartbeat of American Music.

Straight Eighths are even and clock like "tic toc tic toc (1 + 2 + 3 + 4 +).

Swing Eighths are a heartbeat "lub Dub lub Dub"(1 -let2 -let3 -let4 -let).

Swing Feels can be indicated at the beginning of the tune with the Swing Indicator telling the musician to play all Eighths as Swing Eights or all Dotted Eighth Sixteenth pairs as Swing Eights.

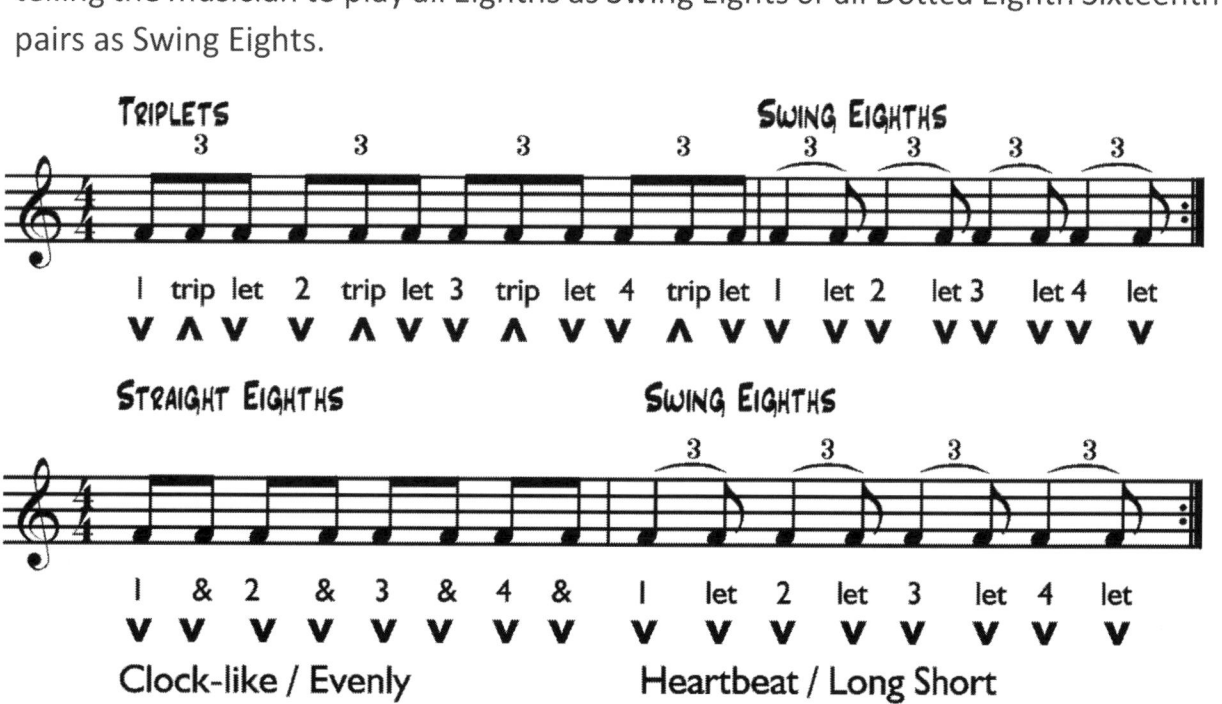

SWING INDICATORS

TRIPLETS ... **SWING EIGHTHS**

1 trip let 2 trip let 3 trip let 4 trip let 1 let 2 let 3 let 4 let

STRAIGHT EIGHTHS ... **SWING EIGHTHS**

1 & 2 & 3 & 4 & 1 let 2 let 3 let 4 let

Clock-like / Evenly   Heartbeat / Long Short

Moveable Power Chords

Press the 6th string, first fret F note with the side of your 1st finger and add the 3rd finger two frets higher on the fifth string note C. Flop the first finger to touch the higher strings to silence them but do not press hard. The A type E string bass note can be fingered or muted. Do not leave strings open.

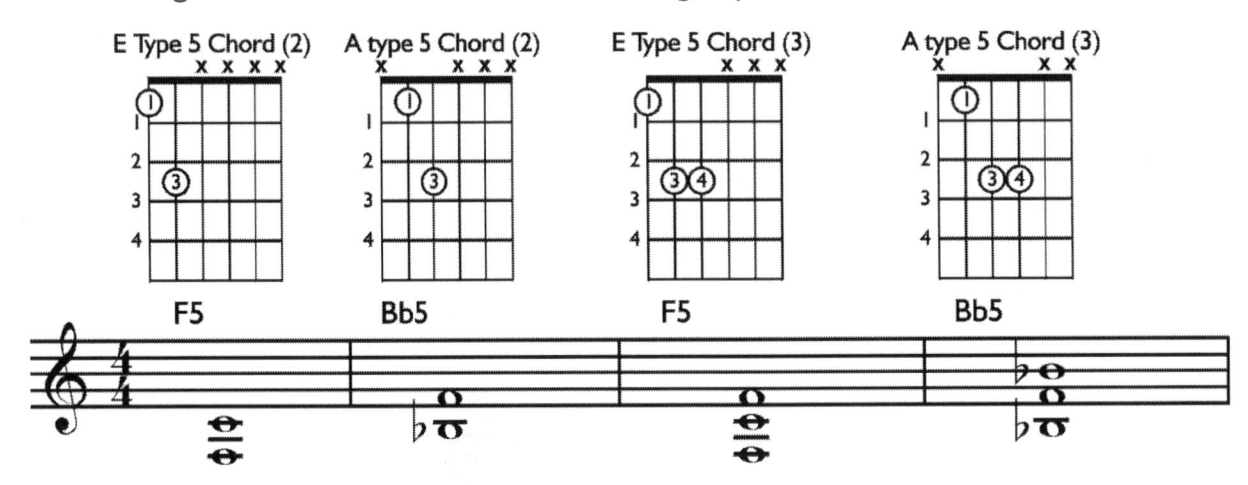

E Type 5 Chord (2)   A type 5 Chord (2)   E Type 5 Chord (3)   A type 5 Chord (3)

F5   Bb5   F5   Bb5

Sixteenth Notes

The count is 1 e & a, 2 e & a, 3 e & a, 4 e & a. The picking is always down / up. These double beam or flag notes make the groove happen in Funk and R & B. Counting sixteenth rhythms is one of the most rewarding challenges of music.

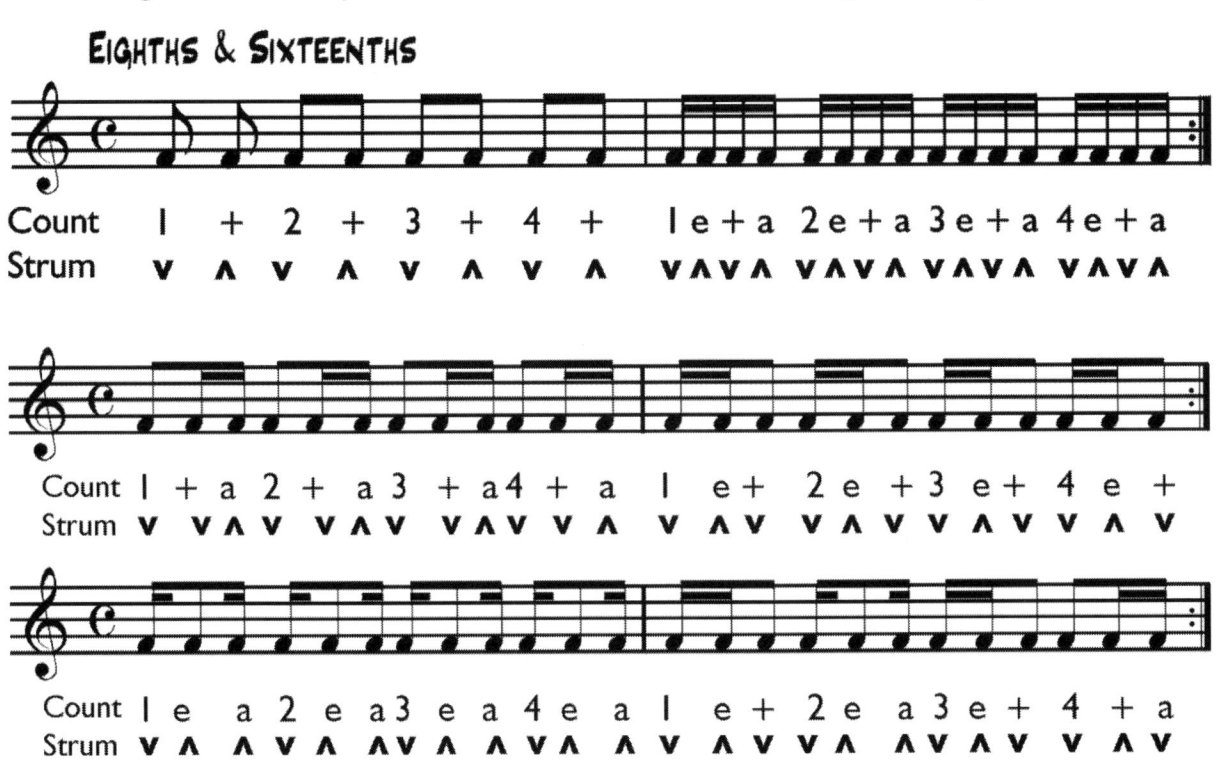

Eighths & Sixteenths

Count   1 + 2 + 3 + 4 +   1 e + a 2 e + a 3 e + a 4 e + a
Strum   V ∧ V ∧ V ∧ V ∧   V∧V∧ V∧V∧ V∧V∧ V∧V∧

Count   1 + a 2 + a 3 + a 4 + a   1 e + 2 e + 3 e + 4 e +
Strum   V V∧V V∧V V∧V V∧V   V ∧V V∧V V∧V V∧V

Count   1 e a 2 e a 3 e a 4 e a   1 e + 2 e a 3 e + 4 + a
Strum   V ∧ ∧V ∧ ∧V ∧ ∧V ∧ ∧   V ∧V V∧V ∧V∧ V ∧ V

Rests and Left-hand Muting

The Chicken Principle The lethal and stupid game of "chicken" can be an analogy for how to move the fretting hand. The car vs pedestrian version is best. The pick is the car. The fingers are the pedestrians. Jump out of the way at the very last moment. Jump in at the very last moment.

This creates a "legato" or long sound. Each note rings for its entire time value. The opposite of this sound is called "staccato" or short. Each note is immediately muted after being struck.

Make the movements of both hands as simultaneous as possible. Play slowly and keep the notes ringing as long as possible. Legato is hard to do while staccato is almost too easy.

Rests are moments of silence. There are rests for every size note from whole notes of silence. sixteenth and even smaller.

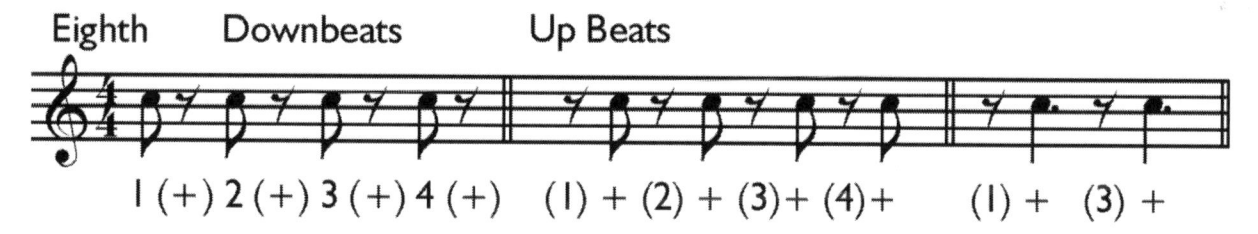

Whole   1 2 3 4   (1 2 3 4)

Half   1 2 (3 4)   1 (2) 3 (4)   **Quarter**   (1) 2 (3) 4

Eighth   **Downbeats**   1 (+) 2 (+) 3 (+) 4 (+)   **Up Beats**   (1) + (2) + (3) + (4) +   (1) + (3) +

Sixteenth

1 e (+a) 2 e (+a) 3 (e) +a 4 (e) +a   (1 e)+ a (2e)+a 3 e (+)a 4 e (+)a

Rests can be made by either hand. Left hand muting is the best technique for making a rest but touching or slapping with the right hand works too.

Palm muting is usually more of a special effect using the heel of the hand resting on the bridge.

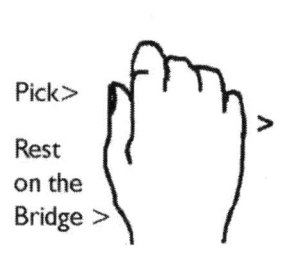

Pick>

Rest on the Bridge >

Muting

For chords such as D, E or A or any chord with lower open strings, extend the pinky or 4th finger across the fingerboard and touch the strings to stop the vibrations: the **Pinky Mute**. For chords such as G, C, or any chord with open interior strings, release the pressure on the strings without lifting off and let the fingers relax and fall over onto the open strings: the **Fall Over Mute**! For bar chords and single notes, leave the finger(s) in place and release the pressure but don't lift to create the silence: **Don't Squeeze Mute**.

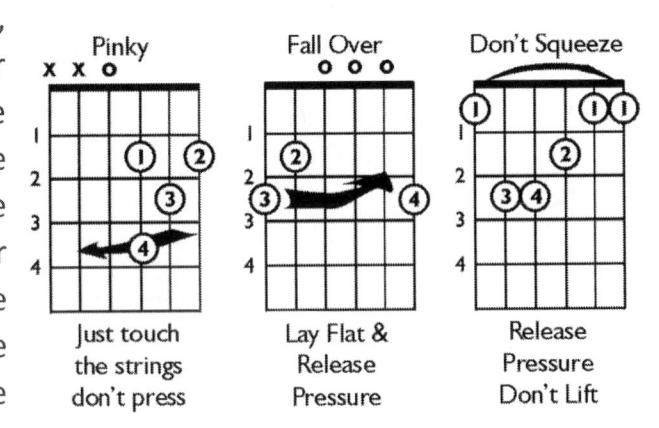

Boom-chuck with kick-snare is the most common usage of these muting techniques. When the kick drum is on beat 1 the guitar plays bass note, the boom. When the snare drum will hit on beats 2 and 4, the back beat, the fingers play the chord. Bass note is the boom. The fingers play the "chuck." Mute immediately after the strum, creating a staccato chord. Mute the chord as it is struck making a percussive sound a "chick."

Expression and More Musical Symbols

Dynamics basically means volume and energy. Playing louder is easier than playing softer. Just as playing slower is harder than playing faster. Do not confuse the two things. When finger picking, the rest stroke can be much louder than the free stroke. More pressure on the string before release increases the volume.

While using a pick loosen your grip on the pick a little bit and the volume will go down. How tightly you hold the pick determines the volume.

Dynamics

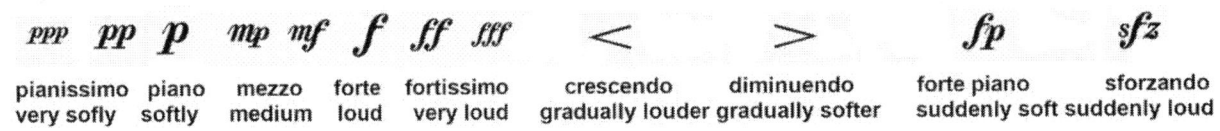

ppp	*pp*	*p*	*mp*	*mf*	*f*	*ff*	*fff*	<	>	*fp*	*sfz*
pianissimo very softly	piano softly		mezzo medium	forte loud		fortissimo very loud		crescendo gradually louder	diminuendo gradually softer	forte piano suddenly soft	sforzando suddenly loud

C/Am Pentatonic Scale

The pentatonic scale has five tones. It is central to all styles of American music. The C pentatonic skips the F and B notes, the 4th and 7th. In the Am pentatonic the B and F would be the 2nd and 6th.

The F and Dm chords share a pentatonic scale: FGACD

And the G and Em chords share the G major or E minor pentatonic scale: EGABD.

All notes are part of the seven-tone diatonic C major scale and the key of C and Am.

Triads have three notes, pentatonic scales have five notes and are made of the relative major/minor chords plus one note.

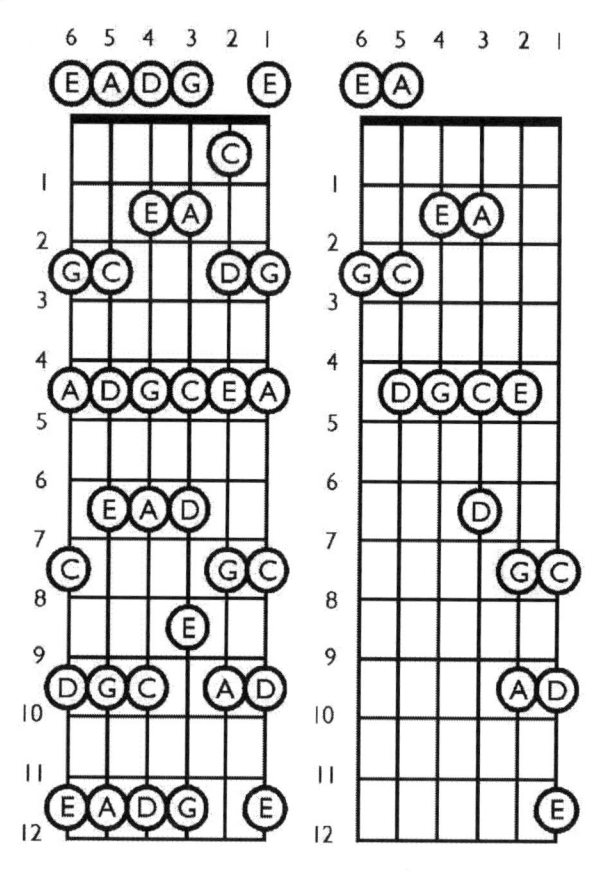

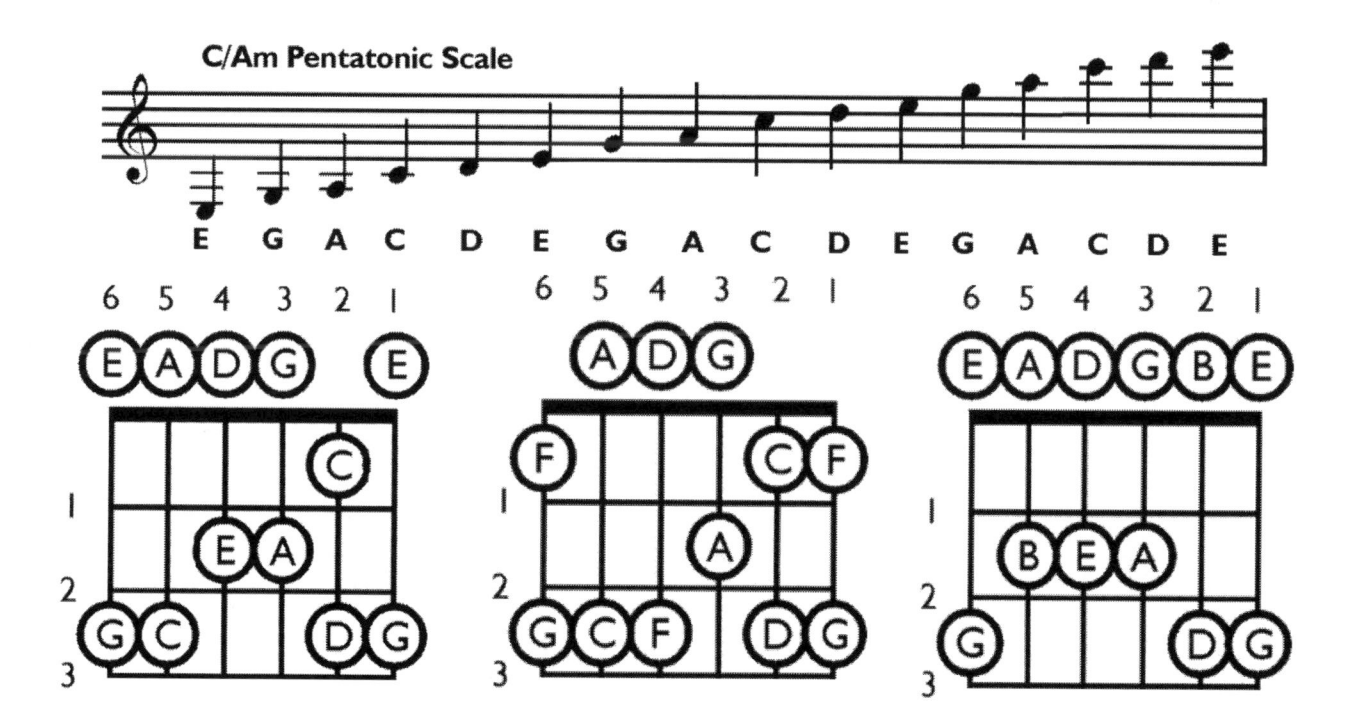

C/Am Pentatonic Scale

E G A C D E G A C D E G A C D E

Folksinger 101 Basic Guitar Skills

Seventh Chords

Chords are stacks of notes. Three notes are called triads. Four notes are called sixth or seventh chords. In a seventh chord, the chord tones are every other note. 1357

Triads: 1 (root) 3rd and 5th   **Seventh Chords: 1 (root) 3rd, 5th, and 7th.**

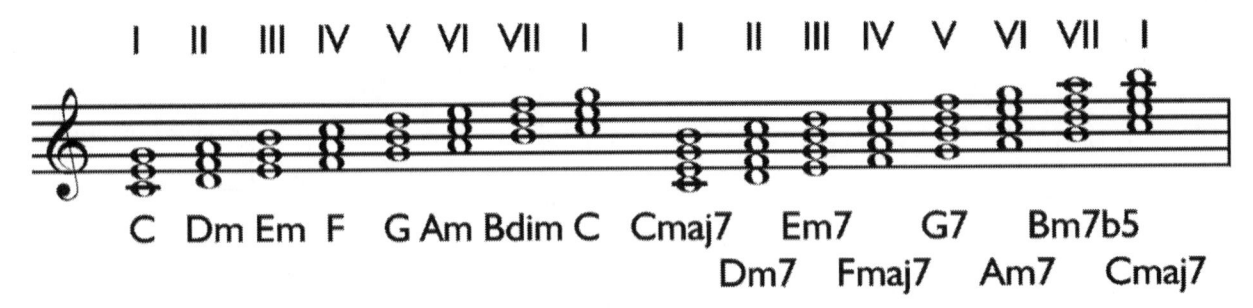

I II III IV V VI VII I   I II III IV V VI VII I

C Dm Em F G Am Bdim C   Cmaj7 Em7 G7 Bm7b5
                          Dm7 Fmaj7 Am7 Cmaj7

In all major keys, the **I** and **IV** chords are major 7th (maj7), the **II**, **III** and **VI** are minor 7th (m7), the **V** is a dominant 7th (7) and the **VII** is a half diminished or minor 7th flat 5 (m7b5). These basic stacks are easy to play on a piano but tough on guitar.

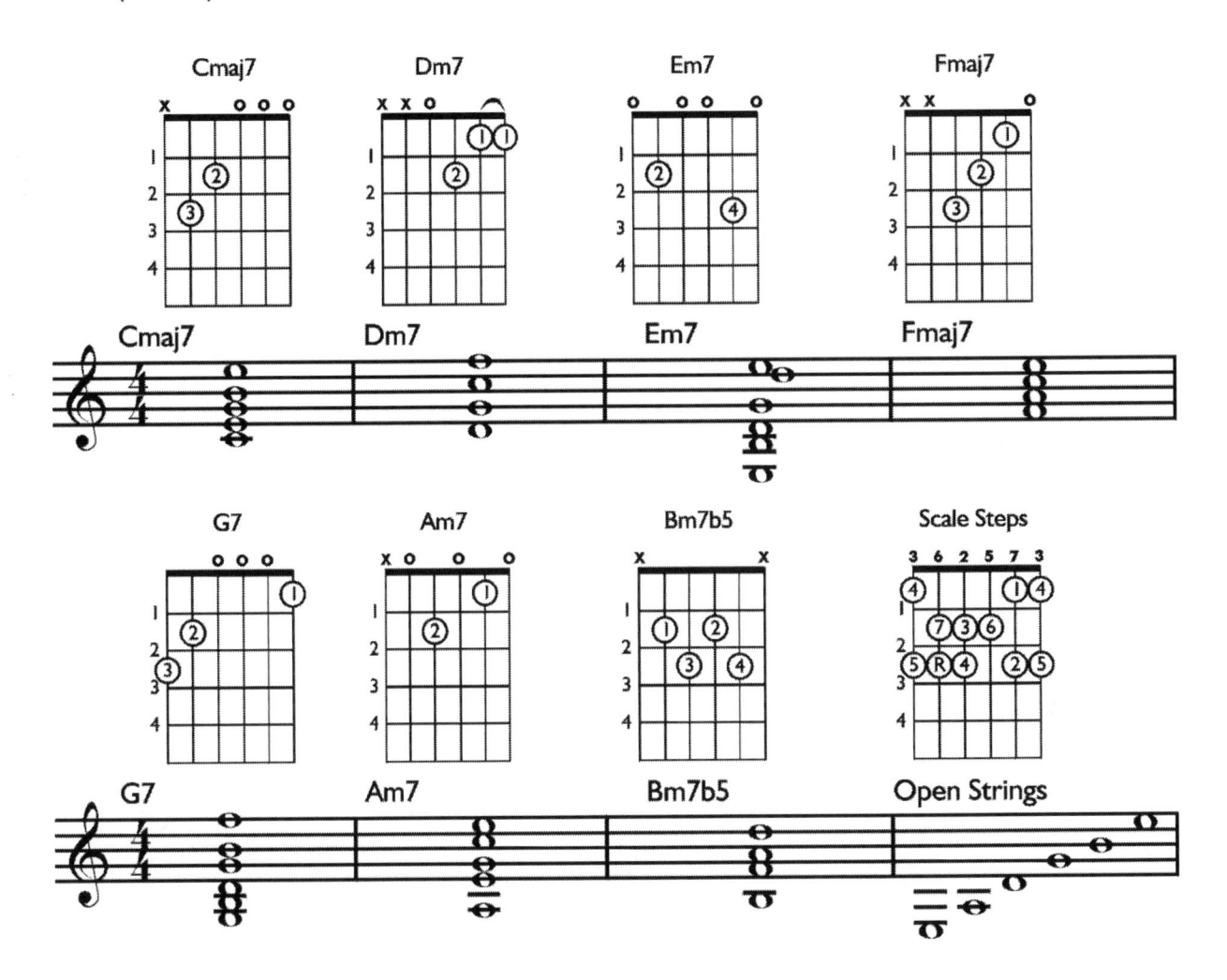

Cmaj7   Dm7   Em7   Fmaj7

Cmaj7   Dm7   Em7   Fmaj7

G7   Am7   Bm7b5   Scale Steps

G7   Am7   Bm7b5   Open Strings

Passing Chords and Inversion

A 1st inversion chord has the 3rd of the chord as the bass note instead of the root note. In between the I and the VIm chord we can place a 1st Inversion V chord.

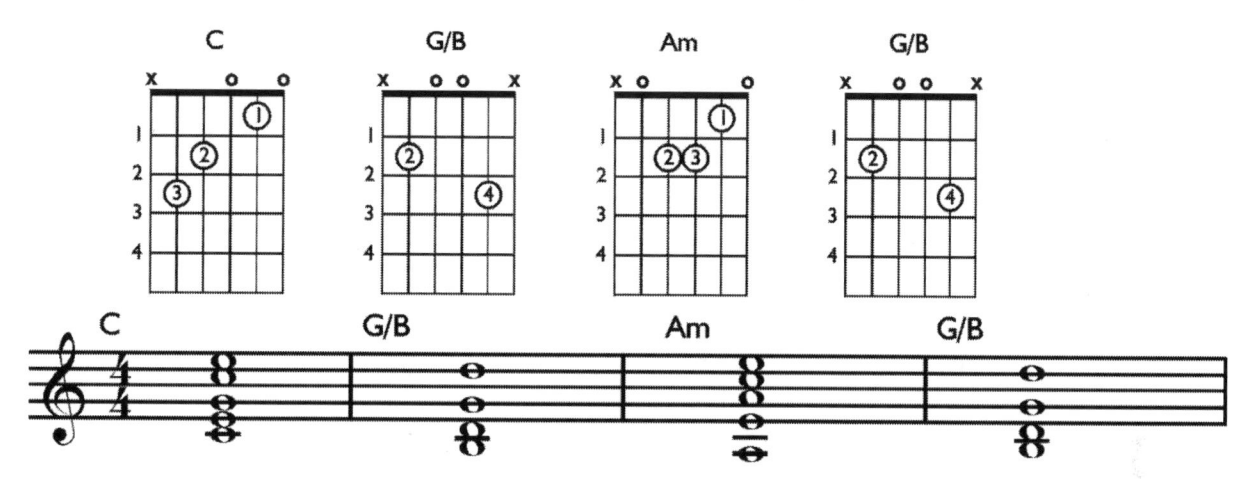

This provides the alphabetical bass line walk down/up with a chord sound which emphasizes the steppingstone effect of the bass line. The Dm/F chord previously mentioned is also a 1st inversion chord, it's just minor instead of major.

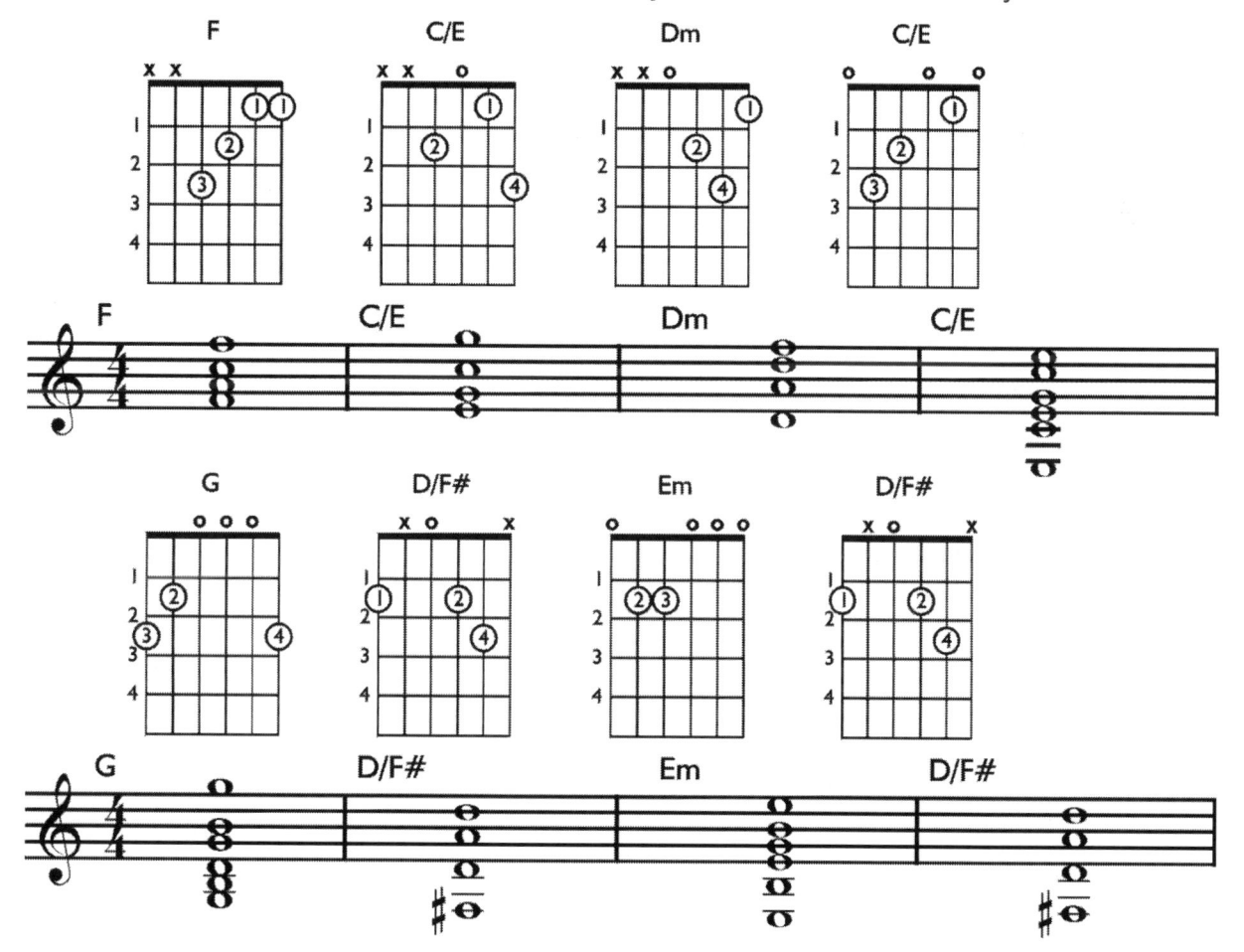

Folksinger 101 Basic Guitar Skills

Popular Rhythms

Every musical style has its own rhythmic vocabulary.

Rock has a heavy back beat, beats 2 & 4. The "and of two" gets accented a lot in pop, rock & folk. Rock shuffles are accented on beats 2 & 4. Swing is accented on the "one".

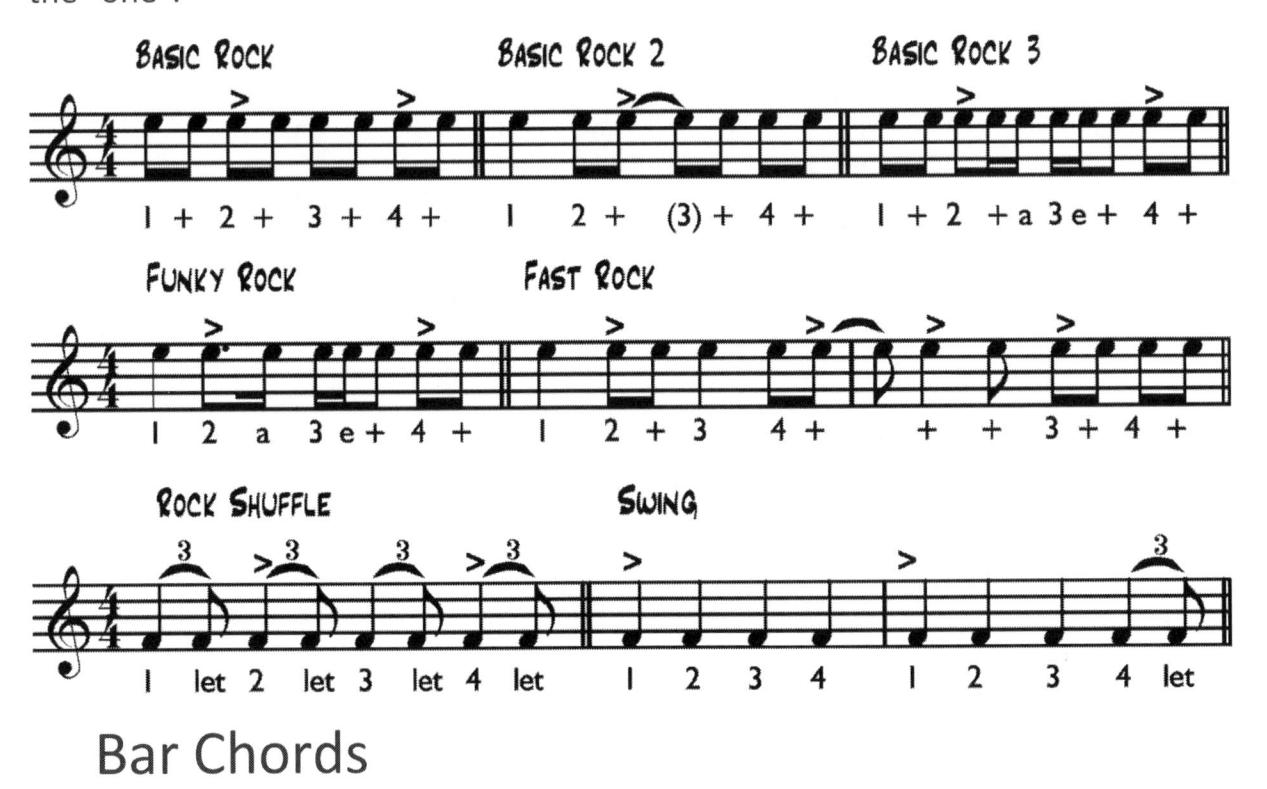

Bar Chords

E type: Root on E String The shape of the chord looks like "E" something.

A Type: Root on A String The shape of the chord looks like "A" something.

The F chord we have learned is really the upper part of the "E" shape bar chord.

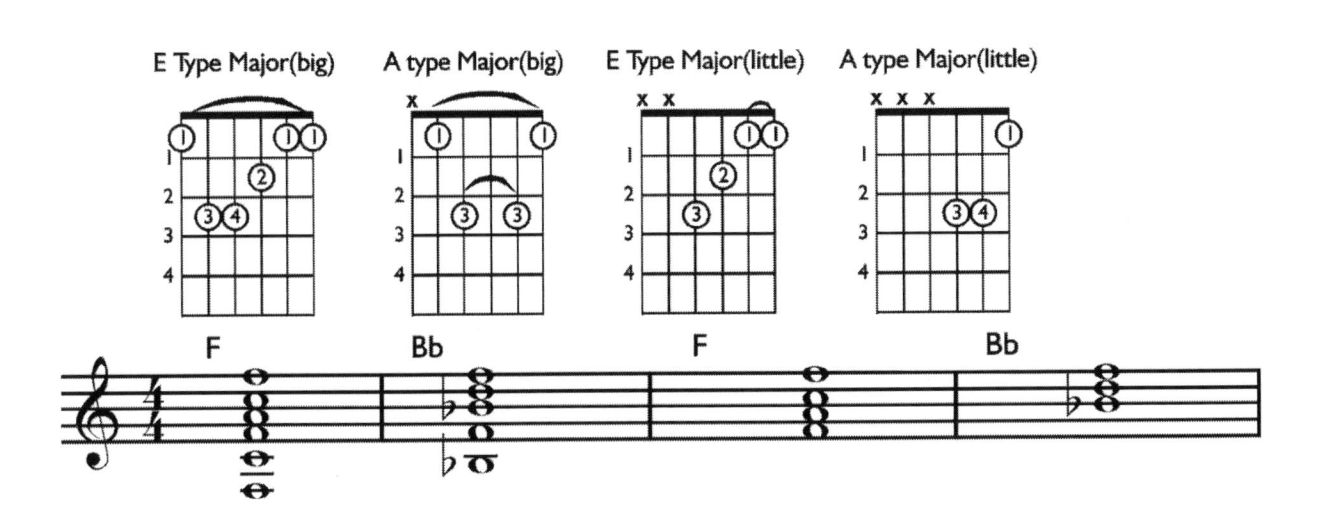

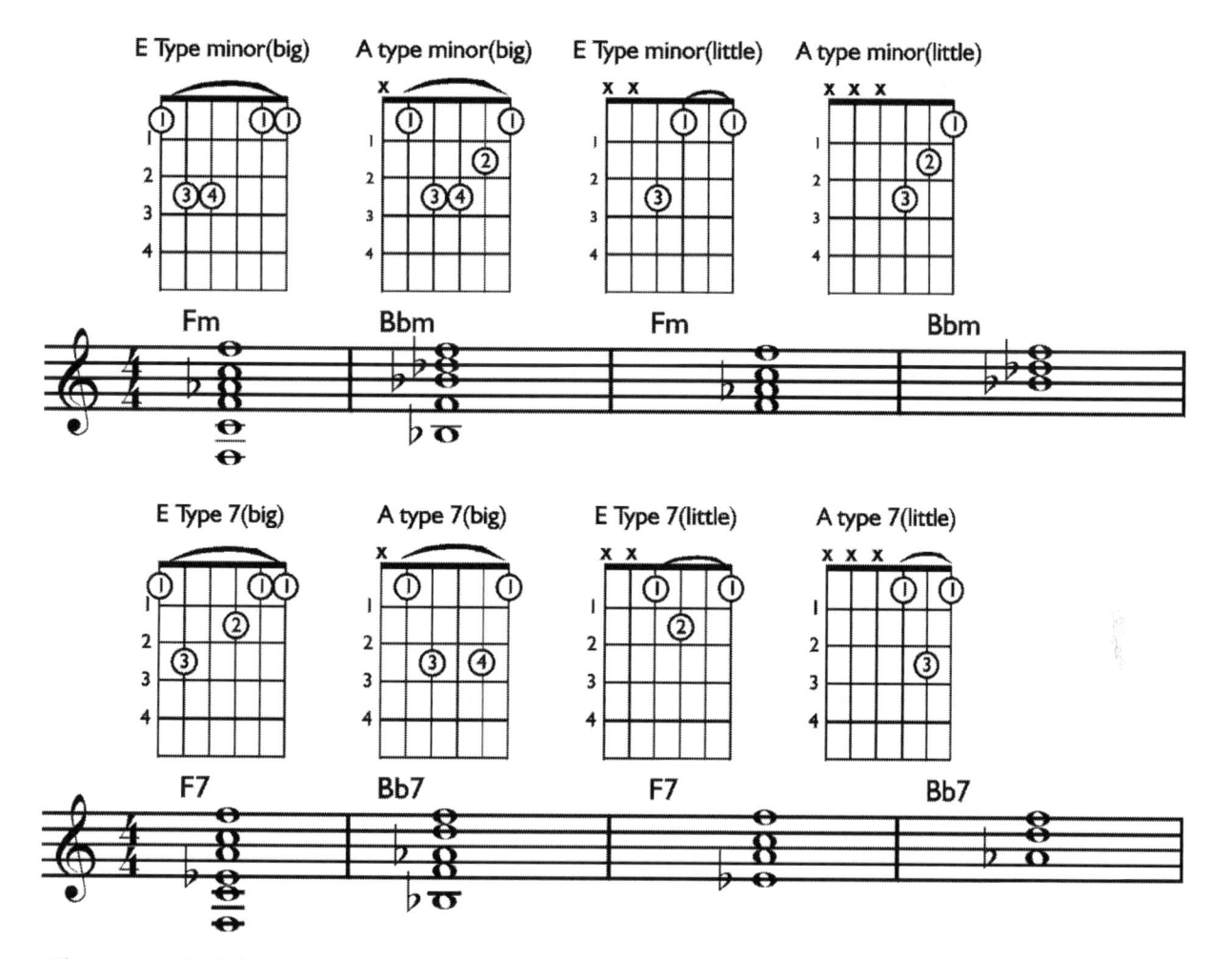

(Chord diagrams: E Type minor(big), A type minor(big), E Type minor(little), A type minor(little) — labeled Fm, Bbm, Fm, Bbm with staff notation)

(Chord diagrams: E Type 7(big), A type 7(big), E Type 7(little), A type 7(little) — labeled F7, Bb7, F7, Bb7 with staff notation)

These and all bar chords can be created using a capo (a fake finger).
It's also good exercise to play between "big" and "little" shapes.

Three Ways to Learn a Song

Show it to me, show me where to move my hands. Learn to watch people move their hands and copy them to understand what they are playing. If you know the neck map and recognize the chords or the notes being played, you can understand the key they are in and play along.

Reading chord charts and music notation. Learn the time signatures, key signatures, and traffic signals such as repeats, DC, DS, and the coda. Chord symbols and the neck map for note reading, bar chords and capo use.

Playing-by-ear or listening closely and figuring it out. Some songs are so simple it seems weird to write it down but a basic chord chart with time signature should be worked up for every tune you learn.

Folksinger 101 Basic Guitar Skills

Finding the Notes

Playing Tunes by Ear and Transcription

If you can sing a song in tune with your guitar you can find the notes you are singing on the guitar and play them. Playing the melody on the guitar and singing along can help you learn to sing the song better.

Rhythm Melody Harmony
Beat Tune Changes

Many common melodies or tunes are easy to recognize, hum & play. This goes for riffs and licks too. The easiest tunes to figure out are folk songs, kids' songs, and Christmas carols. Here are the first four notes of "Silent Night" figure it out and transcribe the rest.

By the way, the same notes to a different rhythm, are also "Rudolph, the Red Nosed Reindeer." "Silent Night" is one, (two) and three one. Beat two is silent. How does the "Rudolph" rhythm work?

Writing down the music in notation is called transcription. The first element of music is rhythm or the beat. What is the count and division? Sing the count instead of the lyrics.

If you can already play and sing the song play it and sing the first note. That note is in the chord you are playing under it. Pick each string, listening for the starting note of the melody.

If you can't tell right away which note it is, sing the tune from each chord tone in turn. When it works, you have found the first clue. If it doesn't, try a different note or chord in the key.

There are only seven alphabetical notes in any key. Let's say you found a G. Above G are A, B, and C. Below are F, E, and D. Sharps or flats may happen, of course, but usually are not combined.

Only three possible things can happen from any note. The next note will be either:
1) the same note
2) higher in pitch (up the musical alphabet!)
3) lower in pitch (down the musical alphabet!)

If it does move up, try the next note in alphabetical order and then the next, if it does not sound correct. If it is lower, try the next note lower on the musical alphabet and the next. Sometimes the next note is just a half step or whole step, one fret or two, away. Sometimes it is a jump or a leap of a third or more.

What if it is a completely new song to you? First, what is the beat count, the rhythm? Is the tune in a major or minor key? Does it sound like good guy theme music or bad guy theme music? Or is it bluesy?

Next, if it is a major key play a C chord. If it is a minor key play an Am. And if it is bluesy, play a G7. Find the starting note in that chord. Each note you discover is a clue to the chord being played.

"Inside" means in the key which will sound normal. "Outside" means out of the key, which sounds weird.

The musical alphabet goes in both directions: up and down. Each tune is a musical puzzle!

Folksinger 101 Basic Guitar Skills

Finding the Chords

The Usual Suspects = Stock Changes

Do the chords sound familiar? Most songs do not use complicated chord patterns or weird sounding chords. Most are using the basic three major, three minor and dominant 7 chords common to each key. If you hear major, try a major chord. Is it too low, slide it up the neck, playing only the basic strings of the shape. They may be using a capo or bar chord.

Transcription Get music paper, a pencil, and a recording of the song you want to learn. Remember, If the guitar is not in tune, you will never find a note that matches.

The Prep Work Play the track, listen, clap your hands, count the beat. Determine the time signature, write it down and draw bar lines, four bars per line.

Next, start the track again and count the beat, tap the paper on each beat while counting across the line and down the page. If you hear a chord change place a mark.

If you can tell if it is a major, minor, or dominant seventh chord you can make note that too with a lower case "m" or "7". Some songs use only 2, 3 or 4 chords.

Intro? Verse? Chorus? Bridge? Outro? When you hear it change sections put a double bar line. When you hear it repeat, place repeat signs at the end and beginning of that section. This will be the first ending. Leave a several bars blank for a second ending.

A bridge or interlude are the next common parts using a DC or DS to get back to the beginning of a third verse or chorus section.

How does it end? What is the outro? Is it something new, a repeating chorus or?

We can do this without an instrument in hand. All you need to do is listen, analyze what you hear and take notes! Now we know the beat and basic song form, but we just don't know which key we are in.

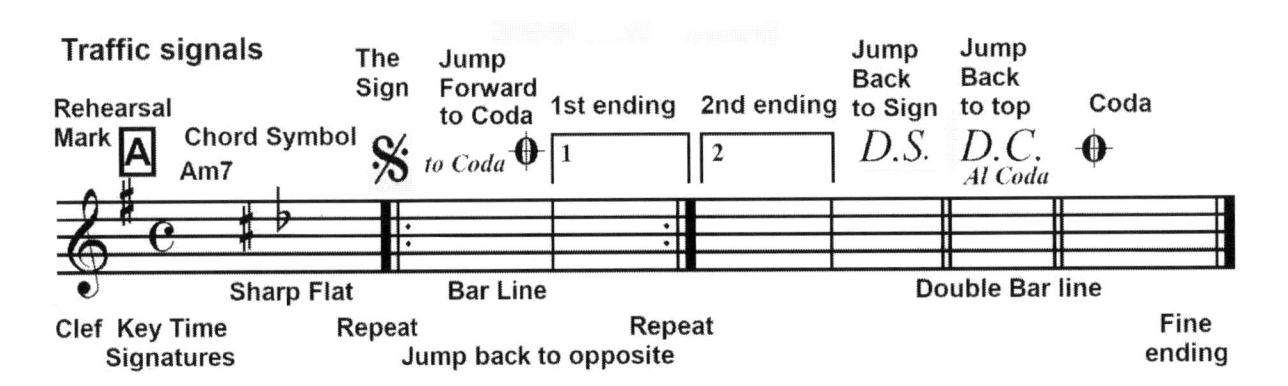

Traffic signals

| Rehearsal Mark | Chord Symbol Am7 | The Sign | Jump Forward to Coda | 1st ending | 2nd ending | Jump Back to Sign D.S. | Jump Back to top D.C. Al Coda | Coda |

Clef Key Time Signatures | Sharp Flat | Repeat | Bar Line | Repeat Jump back to opposite | Double Bar line | Fine ending

Use the bass note rule. The bass note is the lowest note of the chord and is usually the name of the chord! Using a note map search the low strings fret by fret until you find a bass note that works most of the time, especially the first downbeat.

Write down the names of the notes that seem to work the best while looking for the very first bass note. Compare your list with the key spelling charts at the back of the book.

Which key is it played in? Most music starts in one key and stays in that key, changing chords, and occasionally borrowing a chord from a neighboring key. There is a sharp side and a flat side in the circle of fifths.

First, play the notes F and B against the recording. If F and B sound good, you are in the key of C.

If F sounds good but B does not, test Bb. If it works, you are on the flat side of the circle of fifths. Test the Eb next, then Ab, Db, Gb, Cb and Fb.

If B sounds good but F does not, test F#. If F# works, you are on the sharp side. Test C#, then G#, D#, A#, E# and B# may happen too.

If you are on the flat side test the next flat, on the sharp side test the next sharp.

Let's say the bass note is the note A at the 5th fret. So, A becomes the first suspect. The key of A major has F#, C# and G#. The key of Am is no flats or sharps.

Major Key Triads - Sharps

I	ii	iii	IV	V(V7)	vi	vii
C	Dm	Em	F	G(G7)	Am	Bdim
G	Am	Bm	C	D(D7)	Em	F#dim
D	Em	F#m	G	A(A7)	Bm	C#dim
A	Bm	C#m	D	E(E7)	F#m	G#dim
E	F#m	G#m	A	B(B7)	C#m	D#dim
B	C#m	D#m	E	F#(F#7)	G#m	A#dim
F#	G#m	A#m	B	C#(C#7)	D#m	E#dim
C#	D#m	E#m	F#	G#(G#7)	A#m	B#dim

Major Key Triads - Flats

I	ii	iii	IV	V(V7)	vi	vii
C	Dm	Em	F	G(G7)	Am	Bdim
F	Gm	Am	Bb	C(C7)	Dm	Edim
Bb	Cm	Dm	Eb	F(F7)	Gm	Adim
Eb	Fm	Gm	Ab	Bb(Bb7)	Cm	Ddim
Ab	Bbm	Cm	Db	Eb(Eb7)	Fm	Gdim
Db	Ebm	Fm	Gb	Ab(Ab7)	Bbm	Cdim
Gb	Abm	Bbm	Cb	Db(Db7)	Ebm	Fdim
Cb	Dbm	Ebm	Fb	Gb(Gb7)	Abm	Bbdim

Minor Key Triads - Sharps

i	ii	III	iv	v(V7)	VI	VII
Am	Bdim	C	Dm	Em(E7)	F	G
Em	F#dim	G	Am	Bm(B7)	C	D
Bm	C#dim	D	Em	F#m(F#7)	G	A
F#m	G#dim	A	Bm	C#m(C#7)	D	E
C#m	D#dim	E	F#m	G#m(G#7)	A	B
G#m	A#dim	B	C#m	D#m(D#7)	E	F#
D#m	E#dim	F#	G#m	A#m(A#7)	B	C#
A#m	B#dim	C#	D#m	E#m(E#7)	F#	G#

Minor Key Triads - Flats

i	ii	iii	IV	V(V7)	vi	vii
Am	Bdim	C	Dm	Em(E7)	F	G
Dm	Edim	F	Gm	Am(A7)	Bb	C
Gm	Adim	Bb	Cm	Dm(D7)	Eb	F
Cm	Ddim	Eb	Fm	Gm(G7)	Ab	Bb
Fm	Gdim	Ab	Bbm	Cm(C7)	Db	Eb
Bbm	Cdim	Db	Ebm	Fm(F7)	Gb	Ab
Ebm	Fdim	Gb	Abm	Bbm(Bb7)	Cb	Db
Abm	Bbdim	Cb	Dbm	Ebm(Eb7)	Fb	Gb

Folksinger 101 Basic Guitar Skills

If it is major try the major one, four and five chords: A, D and E and relative minors: F#m, Bm and C#m.

If it is minor try the minor one, four five chords: Am, Dm, Em or E7 and relative majors: C, F, and G.

A capo can let you play any key using the chord shapes of the Key of C and G. Capo the guitar at the first fret and the chord shapes of the key of G become Ab and key of C becomes Db.

Capo the guitar at the second fret and the shapes of the key of G major become the key of A major. C major becomes D major.

Capo the guitar at the third fret and key of G becomes Bb and key of C becomes Eb.

Are there descending or ascending basslines?
Is the chord above that bass note major or minor or dominant seventh?
Does it sound like a major chord to relative minor?
Or a one-five like C to G7 or D to A7? Or any of the chord patterns like "the oldies". Generally, is the song in a major key or minor key or is it bluesy (Dom 7)?

What if some chords do not work? The C is also in the key of G and F. If there are three major chords in a key, then any major chord can be in three different keys.

And because the G and F chords have their own keys, chords from the key of G or the key of F can be borrowed.

This adds the key of G's D, D7, Bm & B7 to our key of C major suspect list along with the key of F's Gm, C7, Bb & A7.

D7 is the five of five, G. Bb is the four of four, F.

Because the Dm and Em chords are in the key of Am, any chords from the key of Dm or the key of Em could happen too. That means that the key of Dm's Gm, Bb & A7 along with the key of Em's Bm, B7 & D chords are on our list.

The Usual Suspects

Chord	I	IV	V	V7
	C/Am	F/Dm	G/Em	(G7/E7)

Chord	I	IV	V	V7
	G/Em	C/Am	D/Bm	(D7/B7)

Chord	I	IV	V	V7
	F/Dm	Bb/Gm	C/Am	(C7/A7)

Keys / The Circle of 5ths

Keys other than C/Am are made by flatting (b) or sharping (#) certain notes to keep the major scale pattern of intervals: whole - whole - half - whole - whole - whole - half. Half steps between 3 & 4 and 7 & 8.

These keys are indicated by a key signature written right after the clef in music notation. Each represents a major key and relative minor key.

Each flat key begins 5 major scale steps down from the root note of the previous key and keeps any flats it had. A new flat is added at the 4th step.

Each sharp key begins 5 major scale steps up from the root of the previous key and keeps the sharps. A new sharp is added at the 7th step.

The Keys of Db & C#, Gb & F# and Cb & B are enharmonic keys.

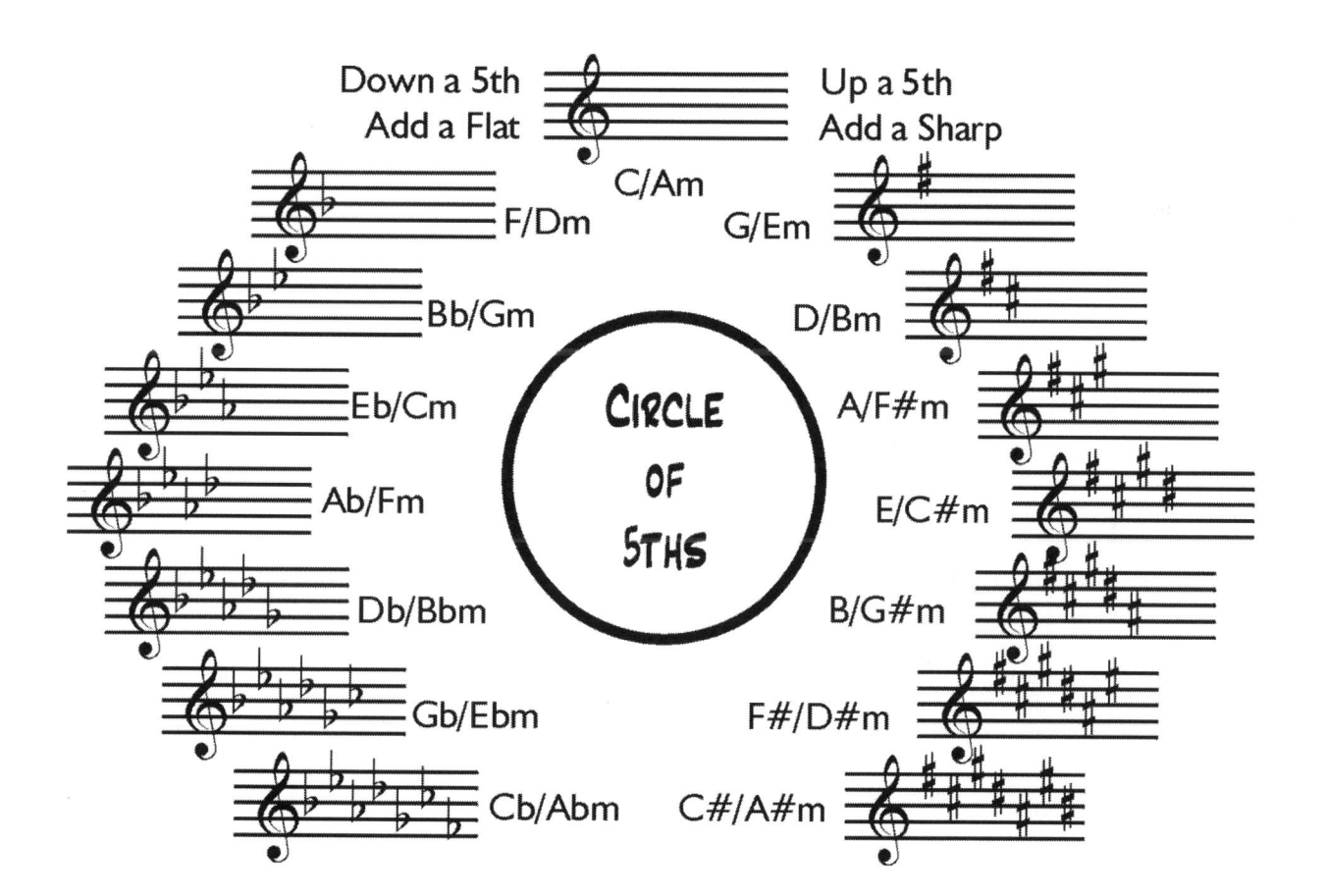

Down a 5th — Add a Flat

Up a 5th — Add a Sharp

Circle of 5ths:
- C/Am
- F/Dm
- Bb/Gm
- Eb/Cm
- Ab/Fm
- Db/Bbm
- Gb/Ebm
- Cb/Abm
- C#/A#m
- F#/D#m
- B/G#m
- E/C#m
- A/F#m
- D/Bm
- G/Em

Folksinger 101 Basic Guitar Skills

The Major Key and Minor Key Spelling Charts

These are complete listings of all the notes in all the keys. Find the key you need along the top row and the scale step number along the side. It looks like multiplication tables from Elementary School for a reason. This information is just as unchangeable and fixed as the multiplication table.

Major Key Spellings

K	C♭	G♭	D♭	A♭	E♭	B♭	F	C	G	D	A	E	B	F♯	C♯	Chord
1	C♭	G♭	D♭	A♭	E♭	B♭	F	C	G	D	A	E	B	F♯	C♯	Maj
2	D♭	A♭	E♭	B♭	F	C	G	D	A	E	B	F♯	C♯	G♯	D♯	Minor
3	E♭	B♭	F	C	G	D	A	E	B	F♯	C♯	G♯	D♯	A♯	E♯	Minor
4	F♭	C♭	G♭	D♭	A♭	E♭	B♭	F	C	G	D	A	E	B	F♯	Maj
5	G♭	D♭	A♭	E♭	B♭	F	C	G	D	A	E	B	F♯	C♯	G♯	7
6	A♭	E♭	B♭	F	C	G	D	A	E	B	F♯	C♯	G♯	D♯	A♯	Minor
7	B♭	F	C	G	D	A	E	B	F♯	C♯	G♯	D♯	A♯	E♯	B♯	Half Dim

These charts have been true for hundreds of years and are best memorized along with the key signatures, time signatures and much of the rest of the musical art.

Minor Key Spellings

K	A♭	E♭	B♭	F	C	G	D	A	E	B	F♯	C♯	G♯	D♯	A♯	Chord
1	A♭	E♭	B♭	F	C	G	D	A	E	B	F♯	C♯	G♯	D♯	A♯	Minor
2	B♭	F	C	G	D	A	E	B	F♯	C♯	G♯	D♯	A♯	E♯	B♯	Half Dim
3	C♭	G♭	D♭	A♭	E♭	B♭	F	C	G	D	A	E	B	F♯	C♯	Maj
4	D♭	A♭	E♭	B♭	F	C	G	D	A	E	B	F♯	C♯	G♯	D♯	Minor
5	E♭	B♭	F	C	G	D	A	E	B	F♯	C♯	G♯	D♯	A♯	E♯	Minor
6	F♭	C♭	G♭	D♭	A♭	E♭	B♭	F	C	G	D	A	E	B	F♯	Maj
7	G♭	D♭	A♭	E♭	B♭	F	C	G	D	A	E	B	F♯	C♯	G♯	7

Final Review

Understanding a system is essential to being able to manipulate it to your own ends. The system of music has a lot to understand but it is not brain surgery, rocket science or nuclear physics. Folk musicians have understood this system for centuries and most of them couldn't even read or write! They could all count and they all knew the ABCs. If you know the alphabet from A to G and can count to thirteen you've got it!

How many measures does 8 bar country or blues have?
What is the primary bass note of an E chord?
What is the secondary bass note of an E chord?
Which notes do we use to walk between two root notes?
What is a hammer-on?
What is a pull-off?
What measure does the "quick change" occur on in the 12-bar blues?
What is a power chord?
What is a power chord's number name and what does it mean?
How many strings are held down by the first finger in the open A power chord?
Which finger plays the "extension" and what beat(s) is it played on?
Which note division is the shuffle related to? Eighth notes or triplets?
How are the beats counted?
Which sounds like a clock? Which sounds like a heartbeat?
What is a "swing Indicator"?
Which fret/string coordinate would you choose to place a movable power chord for the chord Ab5?
Are there any alternative locations?
What is the difference between playing G5 and F5?
What is the difference between playing "I IV V" using movable power chords in the key of G instead of F?
How are sixteenth notes counted?
What beat division does sixteenth notes create?
How many notes are in a triad chord? How many notes are in a seventh chord?
What does "legato" mean? How about "staccato"?
What is a passing chord?

Folksinger 101 Basic Guitar Skills

What is the passing chord between C and Am?
What is the most basic rock rhythm?
What is the most basic swing rhythm?
What are "stock changes"?
Which string has the bass note for the E shape bar chord?
How about the A shape?
How many of the major or minor chords can you now play using bar chords?
What is a quarter rest and how long does it last?
What are the three main left hand muting techniques?
What is the circle of fifths?
What is key spelling?

Variety makes the musician. A good guitarist needs a variety of techniques to change chords, to learn tunes, to pluck strings, to mute strings, to count the beat and to divide the beat. Gather as many tricks as you can for your bag of tricks.

Listening makes the artist. The most dangerous people in the music industry are those with educated ears.
Those who recognize what they are hearing and know what to do and how to do it. These people listen to everything! and they can play anything!

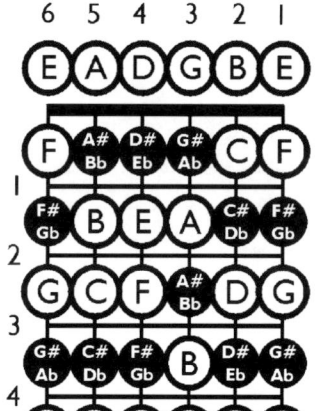

Note Guide for Guitar

Treble Clef Notes and the open position guitar locations

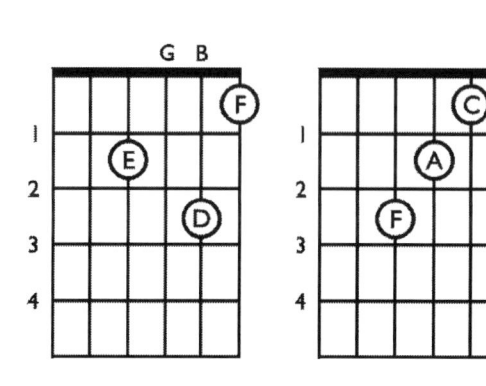

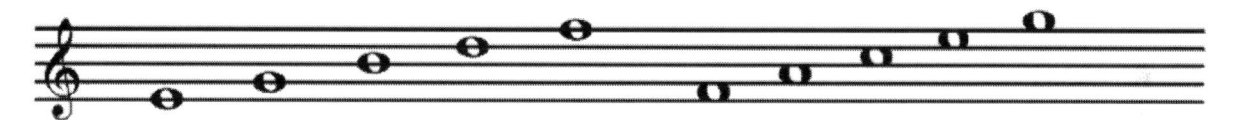

Elvis' Guitar Broke Down Friday   Fat Alley Cats Eat Garbage

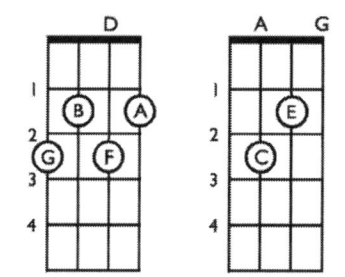

Bass Clef Notes and the open bass guitar locations

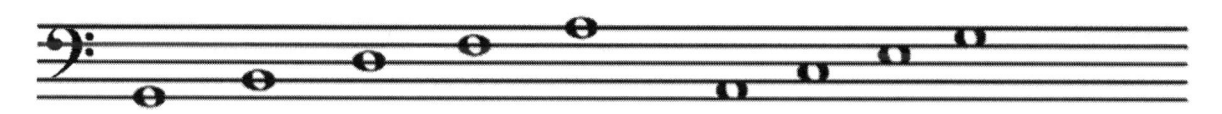

Good Burritos Don't Fall Apart   All Cows Eat Grass

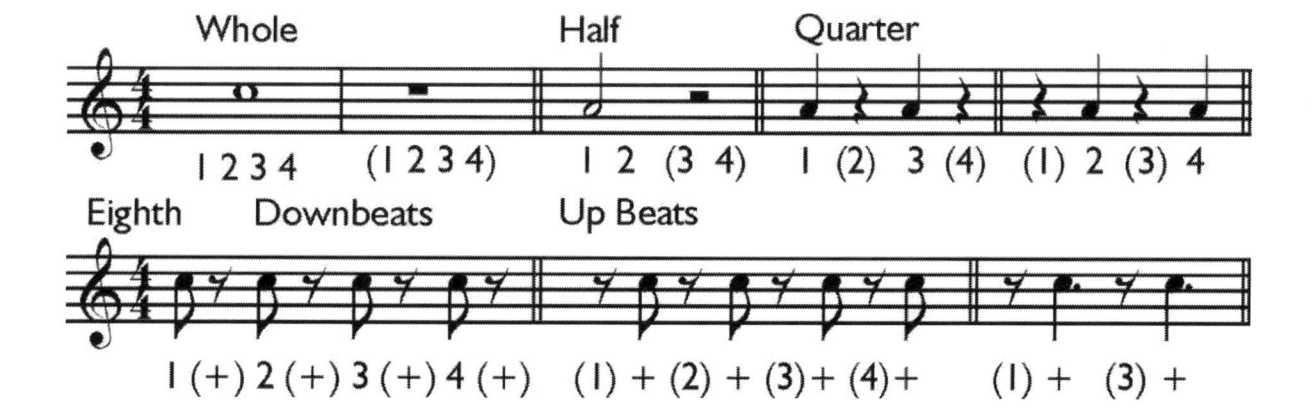

Whole Half Quarter

1 2 3 4   (1 2 3 4)   1 2 (3 4)   1 (2) 3 (4)   (1) 2 (3) 4

Eighth Downbeats Up Beats

1 (+) 2 (+) 3 (+) 4 (+)   (1) + (2) + (3) + (4) +   (1) +   (3) +

Folksinger 101 Basic Guitar Skills

Traffic signals

| Rehearsal Mark **A** | Chord Symbol Am7 | The Sign 𝄋 | Jump Forward to Coda ⊕ to Coda | 1st ending |1| | 2nd ending |2| | Jump Back to Sign D.S. | Jump Back to top D.C. Al Coda | Coda ⊕ |

- Clef, Key, Time Signatures
- Sharp Flat
- Bar Line
- Repeat — Jump back to opposite
- Repeat
- Double Bar line
- Fine ending

Dynamics

| *ppp* | *pp* | *p* | *mp* | *mf* | *f* | *ff* | *fff* | < | > | *fp* | *sfz* |
| pianissimo very softly | piano softly | | mezzo medium | forte loud | | fortissimo very loud | | crescendo gradually louder | diminuendo gradually softer | forte piano suddenly soft | sforzando suddenly loud |

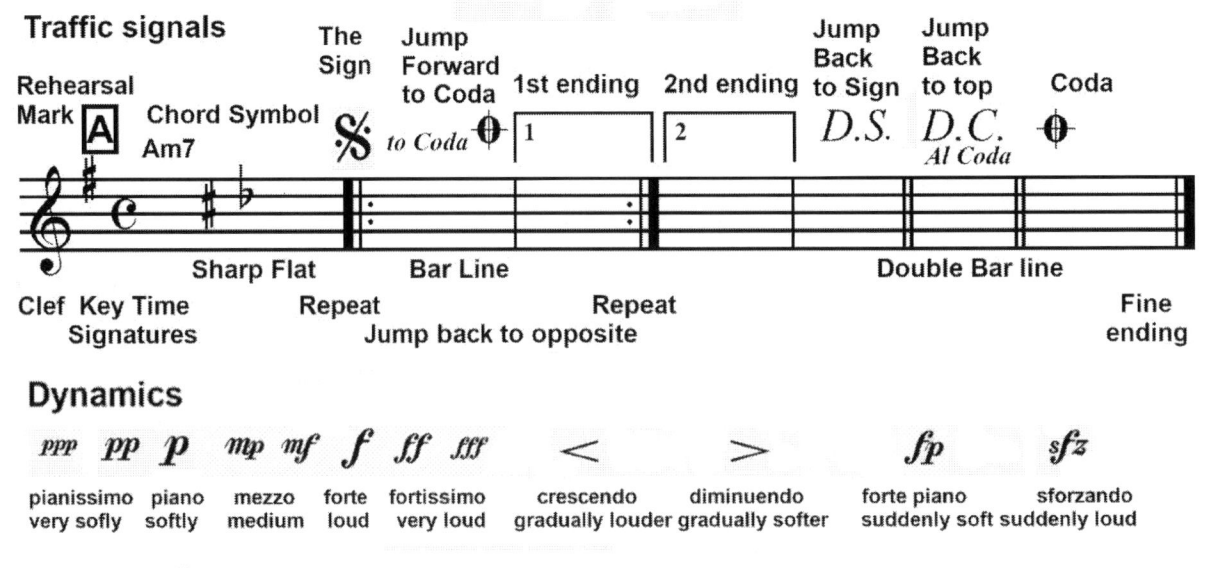

Time Signatures

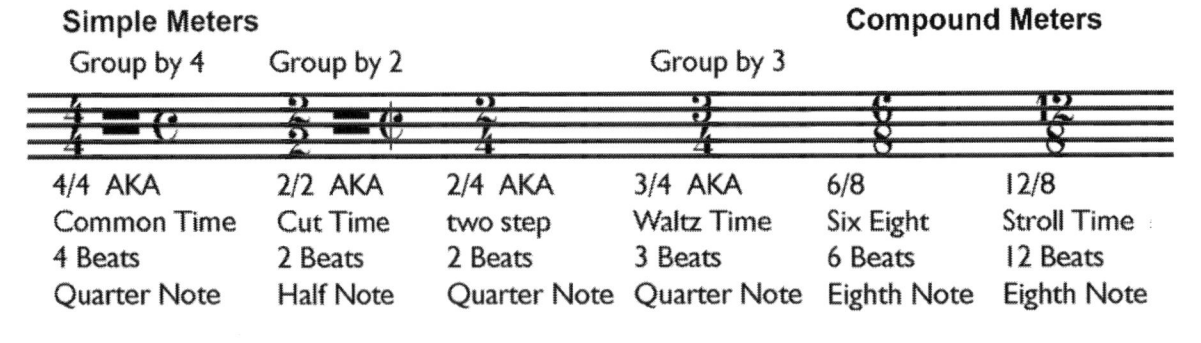

Simple Meters

- Group by 4: 4/4 AKA Common Time, 4 Beats, Quarter Note
- Group by 2: 2/2 AKA Cut Time, 2 Beats, Half Note
- Group by 2: 2/4 AKA two step, 2 Beats, Quarter Note
- Group by 3: 3/4 AKA Waltz Time, 3 Beats, Quarter Note

Compound Meters

- 6/8 AKA Six Eight, 6 Beats, Eighth Note
- 12/8 AKA Stroll Time, 12 Beats, Eighth Note

Key Signatures

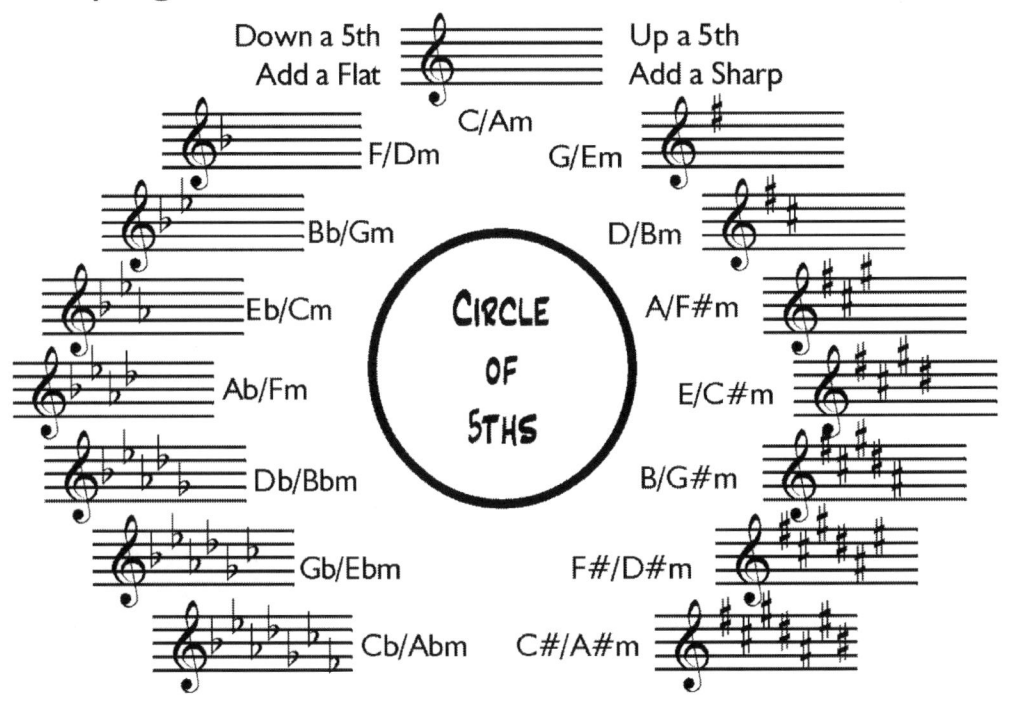

Down a 5th — Add a Flat | Up a 5th — Add a Sharp

Circle of 5ths:
- C/Am
- F/Dm
- Bb/Gm
- Eb/Cm
- Ab/Fm
- Db/Bbm
- Gb/Ebm
- Cb/Abm
- G/Em
- D/Bm
- A/F#m
- E/C#m
- B/G#m
- F#/D#m
- C#/A#m

Made in the USA
Columbia, SC
01 October 2023